Clemens M. Hutter

# GROSSGLOCKNER

## The Dream Road of the Alps
•
## Fantastische weg over de Alpen
•
## Grandiose route des Alpes
•
## La meravigliosa strada delle Alpi

*vcm*
**VCM-Verlag**

## The autor · De auteur · L'auteur · L'autore

Dr. phil. Clemens M. Hutter is a journalist and author of numerous in-depth books on political topics. As an enthusiastic alpinist, he has also been deeply engaged in the cultural and social history of the Eastern Alps. The reference book, "Großglockner – Mule Track, Roman Road, Alpine Highway" and two other books on the "Hohe Tauern" National Park are proof of this interest · Dr. Clemens M. Hutter is journalist en auteur van talrijke boeken over politieke thema's. Als enthousiaste alpinist heeft hij zich intensief bezig gehouden met de culturele en sociale geschiedenis van de oostelijke Alpen. Het standaardwerk „Großglockner – Bergpad voor lastdieren, Romeinse weg, moderne bergroute" en twee boeken over het Nationale Park „Hohe Tauern" zijn hiervan het bewijs · Dr. phil. Clemens M. Hutter est journaliste et auteur de nombreux essais sur des sujets politiques. Alpiniste passionné, il s'est consacré à l'histoire culturelle et sociale des Alpes orientales. Son ouvrage principal «Großglockner – Saumpfad, Römerweg, Hochalpenstraße» et deux livres sur le Parc National «Hohe Tauern» témoignent de ses traveaux · Il Dr. phil. Clemens M. Hutter è giornalista ed autore di numerosi libri su temi politica. Essendo un appassionato alpinista, si è occupato a fondo della storia culturale e sociale delle Alpi orientale. Lo dimostrano l'opera classica «Großglockner – Saumpfad, Römerweg, Hochalpenstraße» e due libri sul parco nazionale degli Alti Tauri.

**English translation by Janet Sorce · Nederlandse vertaling door Nico de Jongh · Traduit par Gérard Marchand · Traduzione di Rachele Cecchini.**

**About the Cover pictures · Foto's op de kaft · Photos de la couverture · Le illustrazioni di copertina**

The title page shows the view from the Franz-Josefs-Höhe onto the northern flank of the Glockner and onto the Johannisberg from where the Pasterze flows into the valley · De voorzijde laat het uitzicht zien vanaf de Frans-Josefs-Höhe op de noordflank van de Glockner en op de Johannisberg, vanwaar de Pasterze naar het dal kruipt · La page de garde montre une vue sur le versant nord du Großglockner et sur le Johannisberg d'où la Pasterze coule dans la vallée depuis la Franz-Josefs-Höhe · L'illustrazione frontale di copertina mostra la veduta dalla Franz-Josefs-Höhe sul fianco nord del Glockner e sul Johannisberg, dal quale scorre a valle il ghiacciaio della Pasterze (Photo / Foto GROHAG).

The pictured marmots on the back page are not shy – not even around visitors · De op de achterkant afgebeelde marmotten zijn niet bang voor de bezoekers · Les marmottes représentées au verso ne craignent pas les visiteurs · Le marmotte raffigurate sul retro di copertina non hanno alcuna paura dei visitatori (Photo / Foto G. Wabnig).

Vertrieb / Distributed by / Distribué par / Distribuito da: Freytag-Berndt & Artaria, Schottenfeldgasse 62, A-1071 Wien, Austria, Tel. 0222/93 95 01, Telex 133 526.

Medieninhaber: VCM-Verlag, Elsbethen. Hersteller: Stiepandruckgesmbh, Leobersdorf. Satz: FERNSATZ, Wien. Verlagsort: Elsbethen.

© 1987 by VCM-Verlag Verena Czezik-Müller, Vorderfager 27, Elsbethen, A-5026 Salzburg-Aigen, Austria. Nachdruck oder Vervielfältigung – auch auszugsweise – nur mit ausdrücklicher Zustimmung des Verlages.

ISBN 3-85021-011-1

---

2 ◀◀  *Game in the Ferleiten Valley · Wild in het dal van Ferleiten · Gibier dans la vallée de Ferleiten · Selvaggina nella valle di Ferleiten.*

4/5 ◀  *A Föhnstorm over the Großglockner announces a rapid change in the weather · Föhnstorm boven de Großglockner kondigt een dramatische weersverslechtering aan · Le föhn sur le Großglockner annonce un changement brutal de temps · La bufera di föhn sul Großglockner annuncia l'improvviso cambiamento di tempo.*

# Contents

# Inhoud

# Sommaire

# Sommario

# GROSSGLOCKNER

The Dream Road of the Alps

•

Fantastische weg over de Alpen

Grandiose route des Alpes

La meravigliosa strada delle Alpi

Großglockner-Hochalpenstraße

"Hohe Tauern" National Park – Nationale Park –
Parc National – Parco Nazionale

Kärnten + Salzburg

Tirol (projected – geprojecteerd – en projet – progettato)

0   1   2   3 km

1 : 100 000  (1 cm ≙ 1000 m)

© FREYTAG-BERNDT u. ARTARIA, WIEN

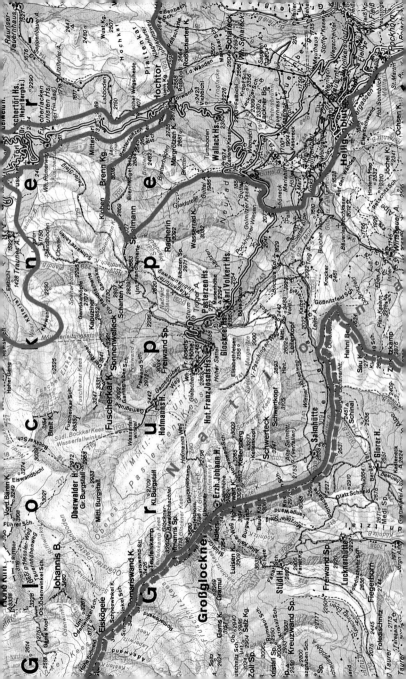

# The Dream Road of the Alps

"Decisive in constructing a man-made road across the Hochtor is the productive, international tourism by those rich people from abroad who are able to spend much money in Austria. To improve tourism, a major road, picturesque and well-situated, is necessary which stands in the foreground next to all of the famous Alpine highways."

With such exacting argumentation, a group of Austrian politicians and officials in 1924 conceived the daring plan to construct the Großglockner Alpine Highway: a small gravel road, three meters wide with a shoulder for passing in viewing range for vehicles weighing up to eight tons. Furthermore, 1,000 workers should build this road through the Hochtor within two summers.

However, these honourable men drafted a castle in the air because capital was lacking. Having lost the 1st World War, Austria had been reduced to one seventh of its imperial size and economic strength. A catastrophic inflation inflicted the country. Nonetheless, the young engineer from the province of Carinthia, Franz Wallack, had been assigned to draft the Glockner Highway project.

Four years passed until the Governor of the province of Salzburg, Franz Rehrl, at the end of 1928 announced a redeeming idea: Usage of the water power from the Hohen Tauern would bring the solution as a huge power plant project of the Berlin-based AEG firm would require a road for construction purposes across the Hochtor. This service road could be later bought from the power company and used as a design model for the Großglockner Alpine Highway. This project, however, failed due to nature as every downpour hopelessly blocked an experimental rainwater gutter with rubble.

## An Idea Takes Form

Consequently, the AEG-"Tauern Plant" was eliminated as midwife for the Großglockner Alpine Highway. This role, paradoxically, was given to the major economic crisis which broke out throughout the world after the crash of the New York Stock Exchange in October 1929 and which drove Austria, already shaken by heavy domestic political crises, once again on a devastating downhill course. This finally induced the decision in 1930 to build the Großglockner Alpine Highway in order to somewhat temper the effect of this catastrophe on the labour market and on the construction industry.

*Fuschertörl against the Großglockner (left) · Fuschertörl met Großglockner (links) · Vue du Fuschertörl en direction du Großglockner (à gauche) · Fuschertörl verso il Großglockner (sinistra).*

A few comparative data illustrate how terribly hard the economic crisis hit the Austrians: from 1929 till 1933 the number of "registered unemployed" rose from almost 200,000 to 557,000 or 26 per cent. The gross national product shrunk from 11,3 billion to 8,8 billion Shillings. 16,400 companies went bankrupt and product consumption fell almost one fifth, for example, in the case of beer from 5,2 million to 3,1 million hectoliters.

The construction of the Großglockner Alpine Highway first received its importance as a measure against unemployment during this oppresively gloomy scenario: for 26 months an average of 3,200 people earned their daily bread through the construction of this road.

On the 30th of August 1930, a group of prominent politicians, tourism strategists, dozens of journalists and an army of curious people gathered in Ferleiten to experience an extraordinary act: along the staked-out line hundreds of explosive blasts were ignited whose thunder even set off a substantial echo in the international press.

In comparison to the "cheap version" which was drafted in 1924 (a small gravel road, three meters wide with passing shoulders in viewing range), the promising official speeches were now for the construction of a mountain highway, six meters wide, for "heavy traffic" which should "technically stand second to none of all the famous Alpine highways". Even the oppressive periods of crisis could not stop the headstrong development of traffic. From 1924 to 1930, the number of private automobiles in Austria doubled to 17,350 (in 1986 there were 2,6 million) and in Germany almost tripled to about 650,000. Moreover, in 1930 the Germans represented almost 53 per cent of the 1,8 million foreign guests in Austria.

The construction of the Großglockner Alpine Highway also allows an impressive view into the social relationships of that time: the weekly wage for 48 working hours was between 52 (for a worker) and 75 shillings (foreman). Black bread cost 58 groschen per kilogram; beef, 3.60 shillings and butter, 6 shillings. A cigarette cost three groschen, a roll, seven; one egg, 14; a half-liter of beer, 48 and a kilowatt of electrical power, 70 groschen. A liter of super gasoline cost one shilling.

A few monthly salaries from those years for comparison: the Federal President, 3,913 shillings; a high school teacher in the highest service category, 730 and a public service employee in the lowest service category, 137 shillings. On the other hand, the Federal President would have had to spend almost two months of salary to afford Austria's most popular automobile of the upper middle class, the "Steyr 100", a 4-cylinder with 1.2 liter cylinder capacity, 32 horsepower, highest speed 100 km/hr. and 9 to 10.5 liters of gas consumption per 100 km. Even the cheapest compact car then cost more than 5,000 shillings – which is understandable considering the ridiculously small output of cars.

# In te domine speravi

On the evening of August 2nd, 1935, a huge fire from the 2,571 meter-high Edelweißspitze announced the completed construction of this Alpine highway. A press release at the opening on the 3rd of August mentioned some impressive figures:

The Großglockner Alpine Highway measured six meters in width and 58.5 km. in length – a 48 km-long continuous highway from Bruck to Heiligenblut, a 1.8 km-long panoramic section from the Fuschertörl up to the Edelweißspitze and a 8.7 km-long glacier road from Guttal to the Franz-Josefs-Höhe. 33.4 hectars of road and parking area were layed out, 67 bridges erected, two tunnels (Hochtor, 311 meters and Mittertörl, 114 meters) built, a 48 km-long road telephone system with 24 emergency phone locations installed and 18 parking areas put up on the most impressive panoramic points.

This project cost 25.8 million shillings; approximately 200,000 shillings less than estimated. As a comparison: a bridge over the Danube built in Vienna also around the mid-1930's (the "Reichsbrücke" which collapsed in 1976) cost 24 million. The total amount of 25,8 million for construction corresponded to around 5 per cent of the entire Austrian investment capital in 1935.

Unfortunately, the construction and maintenance of this Alpine highway also took the life of 20 people. The chapel on the Fuschertörl, designed by Clemens Holzmeister, is dedicated in their memory.

As workers in the summer of 1933 dug out the Hochtortunnel, they found a coin from the time of Empress Maria Theresia in the rubble on the slope of the north side. Wallack had the inscription on this silver piece (In te domine speravi – I have hoped for you, oh Lord) carved in the portals of the Hochtor in gratitude for the successful project, despite all its problems. Of course, this should also serve as an indication of how extremely difficult times promote faith in God.

The Großglockner Alpine Highway had already passed its first test by the 4th of August 1935, the day after its opening: 75 drivers appeared in Fusch for the start of the "1st International Glockner Race" – over 19.5 km. and almost 1,600 meters in altitude up to the Fuschertörl. The victor on this rolled sand road (the entire road was first asphalted in 1939) was the Italian, Mario Tadini, in an Alfa Romeo (racing car class over 2,000 ccm.) in 14:42.74 minutes (79.6 km/hr.).

Afterwards, racing drivers and the press highly praised the road construction engineer Wallack: "The highway is excellently laid out ... completely safe for the fastest driving ... ideally built and first-class ... simply incredible ..." and according to the British "Guardian", a "very meaningful piece of technical achievement".

The automobile industry is profiting up to the present day from this technical achievement. Since its opening in 1935, the Großglockner Alpine Highway is the classical run for testing motors and brakes. If, occasionally, "slow" vehicles with special chassis, peculiar trailers and switched-on blinker lights creep up or down the highway, this means that an automobile company is going to great means to perfect the technical safety of the automobile.

In the summer the motorist's eyes are also caught by those cyclists who verify their stamina on this Alpine highway. Since 1949 the Glockner lap across the Hochtor is the high point of the "Österreich-Rundfahrt" bicycle race. The top performances of these "champions of the highway" allow for an estimate that the fastest time up till now for the ride from Heiligenblut to the Hochtor (52.02 minutes) corresponds to an hourly average speed of 16.1 kilometers.

# Natural Conservation and Engineering

As soon as construction began on this Alpine highway, which, according to Wallack's idea, should "stand second to none of all the Alpine highways", a growing opposition to this project among conservationists had been aroused. In 1918, the wood industrialist from the province of Carinthia, Albrecht Wirth, had bought an area of almost 41 square kilometers around the Pasterze glacier and had given the "Alpenverein" (Alpine mountain association) the duty of "preventing this mountain landscape as a natural conservation area from ever becoming a part of the Alpine tourist industry". However, the Glockner highway should still lead up to the Franz-Josefs-Höhe, a point on the edge of this natural conservation area that offers an unparalleled view onto Austria's largest glacier and highest peak.

At that time, the conservationists did not win out against the urgent demands to create employment. Fortunately, however, Wallack was not only a road construction engineer but also an excellent Alpinist with a sense for natural conservation. Therefore, he gave protection of the landscape a high priority during construction: he saw to it that the plant life within the construction lines was carefully removed to replant it on slopes and other construction scars. He even had plants layed out in various altitude and climatic zones in order to breed that growth compatible with the biotope which would later be needed when expanding and modernizing this road.

There are numerous signs along the Großglockner Alpine Highway requesting tourists to observe natural conservation. Nature lovers respect such regulations as heavy tourism is a great strain on nature, in which and from which we all live.

These are all reasons why the Großglockner Alpine Highway joins into the Hohe Tauern National Park almost unnoticed. The highway cuts through the park between the Fuschertörl and Hochtor as well as from Guttal up to the Franz-Josefs-Höhe.

Thus, the lay-out and staking-out of this Alpine highway, in the opinion of the internationally respected Austrian architect, Prof. Friedrich Achleitner, keep pace with the criteria of our demanding era: "Although it is still completely a product of craftsmen's methods, the terrain could, thus, not yet be violated by the rigorous usage of machines and the beauty of the landscape and its becoming opened are the focal point. This is proof that economic interests and technical knowlege need not destroy a landscape."

## Vestiges from Thousands of Years Ago

This highway across the Hochtor and through the core of the Hohe Tauern National Park follows ancient tracks which left traces of impressive finds.

In the "Beindlkar", south of the Mittertörl (at the 31st km.), a bronze dagger from the 17th centruy B.C. was found next to the road. About two walking hours from this point down the valley, a woodcutter discovered a piece of a pure golden Celtic neck band from the 5th centrury B.C. During construction of the Hochtor (at the 33.4 km.), a worker came upon a Hercules statue and fragments of a

*This small Hercules statue was found during the construction of the Hochtortunnel ·*
*Dit Hercules-beeldje werd bij de bouw van de tunnel door het Hochtor gevonden ·*
*Cette statuette d'Hercule fut trouvée lors de la construction du tunnel du Hochtor ·*
*Questa statuetta raffigurante Ercole fu trovata durante la costruzione della galleria del Hochtor.*

Roman terra-cotta lamp from the time of Christ's birth – along with equally valuable finds in the valleys on both sides of the Hochtor proving that the Romans used this Alpine passage. Furthermore, active trade was conducted in the Middle Ages via this pass as testified by hundreds of hobnails, hoofs, spurs and horse bridle studs which all appeared along the Glockner Highway. Moreover, we know from old documents that at that time almost 10 per cent of all long-distance trade between the trade center, Venice, and the southern German area and Bohemia passed along the route across the Hochtor.

Today's motorists hardly can imagine that the transalpine trade at that time was predominantly carried out in winter since most of the traders "moonlighted" as farmers and had to cultivate their fields. Spiked hobnails which were discovered in large quantities along the route – certainly forerunners of the spike tires for cars – document the winter trade traffic.

Of course, some dismal freight also headed south via the Hochtor. During completion of the Glockner Highway, prisoners chains from the 17th century were found in the "Hexenküche" ("Witches' Kitchen") area at the 23.5 km. At that time, criminals and poachers in Salzburg were usually given a galley sentence and chained to each other as they were driven to Venice across this pass.

At numerous places along the Großglockner Alpine Highway, signs are posted calling attention to the "Römerweg" ("Roman Road") which can be recognized as running parallel to the motor highway for a long distance. These remains of a very cleverly-laid path, up to four meters wide, clearly originate from the Middle Ages, from the Golden Age of transalpine trade on horseback and from the gold rush period in the Hohen Tauern.

The roman author, Polybios (circa 200-120 B.C.), reported what tempted individuals, already in his era, in this highly mountainous wilderness: "Gold, two feet deep, partly pure gold as large as beans" and, in such quantities that "the price of gold in Italy immediately sank one third". In the middle of the 16th century, gold mining reached its climax with yearly yields of up to about 870 kilograms of gold, particularly in the mountains east of the Glockner Highway, still known today as the "Goldberg" group. That was close to 10 per cent of the gold production in the known world at that time and the reason why Salzburg was then also called "Little Peru of the Old World".

Even today, the skillful eye is able to recognize the rubble heaps around the Hochtor from the medieval gold mining. Near the 32.6

*16/17 ◀ Curves around the "Knappenstube" (left) and late-summer snow drifts · Scherpe bochten bij de „Knappenstube" (links) en een sneeuwjacht in de nazomer · Lacets de la «Knappenstube» (à gauche) et tempête de neige à la fin de l'été · Curve della «Knappenstube» (sinistra) e nevischio ad estate inoltrata.*

kilometer, the sign "Knappenstube" ("Miners' Room") refers to a deteriorated tunnel entrance next to the Glockner Highway.

The border between the Austrian provinces of Carinthia and Salzburg passes through the Hochtor. This natural border along the main Alpine ridge also reveals a noteworthy piece of history.

## Man Populates the Alps

As the Bavarians sparsely populated the northern Tauern valleys in the 7th century, they had to cut meadows and fields from the virgin forests. The name "Hochmais" (at the 21.6 km.) gives clear indication of the labourious clearing for cultivation (old High German "meizan" = clearing, hew). The Slavs, living in the Mölltall valley at the time, did similarly as can be gathered from the field name "Laserzen" ("laz" = clearing) or the village Stribach ("strebsti" = clearing). The "Naßfeld" (wet field), on the northern slope of the Großglockner Alpine Highway (26th km.), was absolutely worthless for agriculture and therefore only a point of orientation as was the "Mesenaten" (35th km.) to the south of the Hochtor ("mizinat" = marshy), being the slavic counterpart of the Naßfeld.

Thus, an immense historical dimension is disclosed which demands our respect: approximately 1,400 years ago farmers and shepherds cultivated the Hohen Tauern. When viewing the impressive late Romanesque church steeple in the Glockner village of Fusch, it can be estimated that the spiritual leaders in the Alpine communities settled down in the 12th or 13th century. General compulsory education first reached the Alpine valleys at the time of the Empress Maria Theresia (1740-1780). At least a century later the first doctor established a practice there, too.

Some 200 years ago, there were already people coming in the Hohen Tauern who did not just presume that ghosts, tempestbrewing witches and mythical monsters lived in the desolate places of the high Alps. In former times, only hunters and shepherds ventured up to these heights as well as occasional botanists searching for medicinal herbs in God's apothecary when suddenly scientists became interested in the mountains, too. This was the impulse for the conquering of the Alps and the scaling of their summits.

In 1799, the Carinthian Prince Bishop, Franz Xaver Count Salm-Reifferscheid, equipped an expedition of 30 persons and 13 horses to conquer the Großglockner. Due to adverse weather, the undertaking failed, however in the following year an even larger expedition of 62 persons and 16 horses succeeded in advancing up to the

*The Pasterze is Austria's largest and most intact glacier · De Pas-▸ 20/21*
*terze is Oostenrijks grootste en gelijkmatigste gletsjer · La Pasterze*
*est le glacier d'Autriche le plus grand et le plus régulier · La Pasterze*
*è il ghiacciaio più grande e più armonioso dell'Austria.*

"Adlersruhe" ("Eagle's Rest") within two days. Furthermore, five men finally reached the highest Tauern summit. These two expeditions were financed by Count Salm-Reifferscheid from his own pocket for a sum that would today enable a 20 man mountaineering expedition in the Himalayas for three weeks.

## Snow Masses in the High Alps

Unfortunately, the women dressed in local costumes at the toll booths must request a small sum of the vistors to the Großglockner Alpine Highway as the maintenance and improvement of this road should not only be borne by the taxpayers.

An Alpine highway, in particular, requires an above average expenditure in technical and financial means to fight the often underestimated destructive force of snow, frost, avalanche, landslide or falling stone. This is necessary to maintain the road surface and substructure and to guarantee guests an absolutely safe ride on terrain which is exposed to extreme climatic conditions.

During the winter, around five meters of snow generally fall on the upper stretch of the Großglockner Alpine Highway (between 2,300 and 2,500 meters in altitude). This includes by no means just the amount of fallen snow. On the contrary, greater importance should be placed on the fact that there is hardly ever a wind calm in these heights and that the wind speed reaches almost three times that of the average value in the valley – with top speeds up to 130 km/hr. This explains the colossal snow drifts and the build-up of huge snow cornices which still hang on the ridges in the summer.

Now it is evident why the Großglockner Alpine Highway passes, in certain sections, through snow alleys, even in July. Here winter storms have piled up the snow masses over the road which once, in 1975, reached the record height of 21 meters - a canyon-like road between high-rise buildings.

Technical progress can also be seen in terms of snow removal. From 1935 till 1937, 350 men shoveled 250,000 cubic meters of snow in an average of 70 days in order to get one lane open. Since 1953, the rotation plows developed by Wallack theoretically perform the work of around 1,000 shovelers. Therefore, five rotation plows and 30 workers can now clear 600,000 cubic meters of snow within 25 days from the entire highway lay-out including all the parking areas. The clearance record was made in 1975 with 800,000 cubic meters of snow which would have filled a 250 kilometer-long freight train.

*View from the Hochmais against the Pfandlscharte · Blik vanaf Hochmais in de richting van de Pfandlscharte · Vue du Hochmais en direction de la Pfandlscharte · Veduta da Hochmais verso la Pfandlscharte.*

The revenue from tolls, therefore, does not feed bureaucratic management machines, but rather assures the usage of the given technical state-of-the-art in order to offer an extraordinary touristic experience to the visitors of the Großglockner Alpine Highway.

## The Pasterze

Visitors to the Franz-Josefs-Höhe should not miss an experience which is offered nowhere else in Europe: the absolutely safe and simple walk on the smooth ice of the up to 300 meter-thick Pasterze which is an area of about 20 square kilometers and has a volume of almost 2 cubic kilometers. From the "Freiwandeck" parking lot a funicular, running since 1963, travels 143 meters down almost to the edge of the Pasterze. In a few steps one reaches a quarter, marked off by ropes, on the ice blue glacier where, already in the morning, little rivulets in dozens of water courses gurgle and murmur. Here the visitor experiences one step in the large circulation system of water: the sun melts down the glacier and gnaws at its substance. However, several kilometers further up on the Pasterze there is snow in the summer, too. There one finds the "supply area" of the glacier whose border to the "consumption

area" (pure ice without snow cover) runs at approximately 2,800 meters above sea level.

Heights of around 3,000 meters and more receive almost two-and-a-half times more precipitation than the valleys. Of that amount, 90 per cent is as snow – between six and ten meters annually. Under the influence of heat and the fluctuation of melting and freezing, this mass sinks together to a density of 20-50 centimeters and, within around 15 years, transforms into ice.

It was only 200 years ago that science unraveled the connection between climate and the formation of glaciers. Before that, God-fearing people resorted to explanations which live on today as sagas.

These sagas recount how luxurious mountain meadows once extended where today the Pasterze fills up a huge valley trough. There the Alpine natives were slaves to unrestrained debauchery and carried their blasphemous conduct to the limit by playing nine-pins with butterballs and pins made out of cheese and letting the priest preach to empty church pews. God, vehemently angered, sent a terrible rainstorm which swept away these sinful doings. Then God had a deadly coldness fall down. Thus, the masses of water congealed into a flood of ice so that this place of debauchery would remain covered forever and would teach mankind to where ungodliness leads.

# An Attraction for Millions

In 1924, Wallack estimated that the annual number of visitors to the Großglockner Alpine Highway would be 40,000. At the beginning of construction in 1930, Wallack was already aiming at 120,000 visitors – and for this, earned mocking criticism by sceptical experts. However, in 1938, the third full year of operation, almost 98,000 vehicles with 275,000 visitors had already been counted. Now 280,000 vehicles, the long-standing average, annually use the Großglockner Alpine Highway. Consequently, at the beginning of the fifties, improvements were begun to provide added safety and also to comply with the demands of greater driving comfort. Thus, the road was built from six to a minimum of 7.5 meters wide and in technically-sophisticated sections with three lanes. The curve radii were enlarged from ten to a minimum of fifteen meters and the number of parking spaces increased from 800 to accomodate 4000 vehicles.

Franz Wallack once had the goal of building a road across the Hohen Tauern which would keep pace with all other Alpine highways. Since then, almost 40 million visitors have indicated that Wallack achieved this goal through his dream road of the Alps.

# Fantastische weg over de Alpen

„Het internationale toerisme van rijke buitenlanders, die van zin zijn veel geld uit te geven in Oostenrijk, is van doorslaggevend belang voor de aanleg van een bergroute over het Hochtor (Hoge Poort). Om het toerisme te stimuleren is er een weg nodig met een interessant verloop en veel uitzichtspunten, die alle beroemde bergwegen in de Alpen in de schaduw stelt."

Met zulke pretentieuze argumenten staafde in 1924 een groep Oostenrijkse politici en ambtenaren het vermetele plan om de „Großglockner-Hochalpenstraße" (Großglockner-route) te laten aanleggen: een weggetje uit steengruis van drie meter breed met uitwijkplaatsen net binnen zichtbereik voor voertuigen tot acht ton. En 1000 arbeiders moesten deze weg in twee zomers over het Hochtor aanleggen.

Maar deze eerbiedwaardige heren ontwierpen een luchtkasteel, want er was geen geld. Oostenrijk was immers door zijn nederlaag in de Eerste Wereldoorlog van een imperiale wereldmacht gedegradeerd tot een economische dwerg. Het land ging gebukt onder een verschrikkelijke inflatie. Desalniettemin kreeg de jonge Karintische ingenieur Franz Wallack de opdracht om het project Glocknerweg uit te werken.

Vier jaar later, tegen het einde van 1928, kreeg de minister-president van de provincie Salzburg, Franz Rehrl een lumineus idee: het exploiteren van de waterkracht uit de Hoge Tauern zou de oplossing brengen. Immers, het reusachtige project voor een waterkrachtcentrale van het Berlijnse AEG-concern, vereiste een weg via het Hochtor. Dit project liep echter stuk op de natuur, daar elke forse regenbui een proefkanaal hopeloos verstopte met steenlawines.

Op deze wijze viel de AEG-Tauerncentrale weg als wegbereider voor de Großglockner-route. Deze rol viel nu ironisch genoeg ten deel aan de grote economische crisis, die na de ineenstorting van de New Yorkse beurs in oktober 1929 de hele wereld op zijn grondvesten deed schudden. Ook Oostenrijk, dat toch al erg leed onder ernstige binnenlandse politieke problemen, werd meegesleurd in een diepe depressie. In het kader van het werkgelegenheidsbeleid werd in 1930 tenslotte besloten om te beginnen met de aanleg van de Großglocknerweg.

## Een idee wordt concreter

Wat voor een vergaande uitwerking de economische crisis had op de bevolking kunnen enige vergelijkende gegevens illustreren: van 1929 tot 1933 steeg het aantal officiële werkelozen van 200.000 tot 557.000 oftewel 26 procent. Het bruto nationale produkt slonk van 11,3 miljard tot 8,8 miljard schilling, 16.400 firma's gingen failliet en de consumptie liep met een vijfde terug – bijvoorbeeld bier van 5,2 tot 3,1 miljoen hectoliter.

Pas tegen de achtergrond van dit naargeestige decor krijgt de aanleg van de Großglockner-route reliëf als sociaal-economisch beleidsinstrument: 26 maanden lang verdienden gemiddeld 3200 mensen hun brood bij de aanleg van deze weg.

Op 30 augustus 1930 verzamelden zich in Ferleiten talrijke prominente politici en toeristsiche strategen, tientallen journalisten en een grote schaar van kijklustigen om de buitengewone dramaturgie van de eerste explosie mee te maken: langs het tracé van de toekomstige weg werden honderden springladingen gedetoneerd, waarvan het gedonder zelfs weerklank vond in de internationale pers.

In tegenstelling tot de 1924 ontworpen „goedkope variant" (weggetje uit steengruis van drie meter breed met uitwijkplaatsen net binnen zichtbereik) begon men nu, na het afsteken van optimistische feestspeeches, met de aanleg van een zes meter brede bergweg „voor het grote verkeer", die „technisch alle andere beroemde Alpenwegen in de schaduw zou moeten stellen". Zelfs de deprimerende crisistijd had namelijk de stormachtige ontwikkeling van het verkeer niet kunnen verhinderen. Van 1924 tot 1930 was het aantal auto's in Oostenrijk verdubbeld tot 17.350 (ter vergelijking : in 1986 bijna 2,6 miljoen) en in Duitsland zelfs verdriedubbeld tot 650.000. Dit was van belang omdat de Duitsers in 1930 circa 53 procent van de 1,8 miljoen buitenlandse toeristen in Oostenrijk vormden.

De aanleg van de Großglockner-route verschaft eveneens een illustratief beeld van de sociale verhoudingen in die tijd: zonder toelagen bedroeg het loon voor een 48-urige werkweek tussen 52 (gewone arbeiders) en 75 schilling (voormannen). Een kilo brood kostte 58 groschen, een kilo rundvlees 3,60 schilling en een kilo boter zes schilling (1 schilling = 100 groschen). De prijs voor een sigaret bedroeg drie groschen, een kadetje kostte zeven groschen, een ei 14, een halve liter bier 48 en een kilowattuur stroom 70 groschen. Voor een liter superbenzine moest een schilling neergeteld worden.

Ter vergelijking enige maandsalarissen uit die tijd: de bondspresident 3913 schilling, leraren aan middelbare scholen in de hoogste dienstklasse 730 en een ambtenaar in de laagste dienstklasse 137 schilling. Toch had de bondspresident nog altijd bijna twee maandsalarissen moeten betalen voor het populairste voertuig van die dagen in Oostenrijk, de „Steyr Honderd", een auto uit de betere middenklasse met een vier-cylinder 1200 cc moter, 32 pk, een topsnelheid van 100 km/u en een benzineverbruik van ongeveer 1 op 10. Zelfs het goedkoopste autootje kostte al meer dan 5000 schilling – begrijpelijk als we bedenken dat er van massaproduktie nog geen sprake kon zijn.

# In te domine speravi

Op de avond van 2 augustus 1935 deed een reusachtig vuur op de 2571 meter hoge Edelweißspitze kond van het feit dat de aanleg van deze bergweg was voltooid. Een persbericht naar aanleiding van de opening op 3 augustus vermeldde de volgende cijfers:

De Großglockner-route was zes meter breed en 58,5 kilometer lang – een 48 kilometer lange verbindingsweg tussen Bruck en Heiligenblut, 1,8 kilometer panoramaweg van het Fuschertörl (Fuscherpoortje) naar de Edelweißspitze en 8,7 kilometer gletscherweg van Gutttal naar de Franz-Josefs-Höhe (Franz-Josefs-hoogte). Er werden 33,4 hectare wegdek en parkeerterrein aangelegd, 67 bruggen gebouwd, twee tunnels geboord – Hochtor 311 meter, Mittertörl (middelste poortje) 117 meter, er ontstond een 48 kilomter lang telefoonnet langs de weg met 24 „praatpalen" en er werden 18 parkeerplaatsen aangelegd op de mooiste punten van de route.

De werkzaamheden kostten ongveer 25,8 miljoen schilling, ca 200.000 schilling minder dan oorspronkelijk geraamd. Ter vergelijking: een eveneens in het midden van de dertiger jaren in Wenen gebouwde brug over de Donau (die in 1976 ingestorte „Reichsbrücke") kwam op 24 miljoen schilling. Dit bedrag van 25,8 miljoen schilling kwam neer op vijf procent van alle Oostenrijkse investeringen in 1935.

De aanleg en het instandhouden van deze bergweg kostte helaas ook 20 mensen het leven. Ter hunner ere is een kapel op het Fuschertörl gewijd, die door Clemens Holzmeister ontworpen is.

*Oil painting entitled "Großglockner" by Marcus Pernhart (ca. 1860) · Schilderij "Großglockner" van Marcus Pernhart (ca. 18060) · Peinture à l'huile «Großglockner» de Marcus Pernhart (1860 env.) · Dipinto ad olio «Großglockner» di Marcus Pernhart (ca. 1860).*

Toen arbeiders in de zomer van 1933 de doorgang door het Hochtor groeven, vonden ze op de noordelijke helling een munt uit de tijd van keizerin Maria Theresia tussen het bergpuin. De inscriptie op dit geldstuk (In te domine speravi – op U, Heer, heb ik mijn hoop gevestigd) liet Wallack in de portalen van het Hochtor metselen – als dank voor het feit dat het karwei ondanks alle problemen geklaard was. En misschien ook wel om de wereld te tonen dat zijn godsvertrouwen in deze harde tijden niet aan het wankelen was gebracht.

Zijn vuurdoop kreeg de Großglocknerweg reeds op 4 augustus 1935, een dag na zijn opening: In Fusch stonden 75 coureurs klaar om mee te doen aan de „Eerste Internationale Glockner-race". Deze race ging over 19,5 kilomter naar het Fuschertörl, waarbij het hoogteverschil 1600 meter bedroeg. De overwinning op deze gewalste zandweg (pas in 1939 werd de hele weg geasfalteerd en daardoor heel wat minder stoffig) behaalde de Italiaan Mario Tadini met zijn Alfa Romeo (racewagenklasse met meer dan 2000 cc) in 14:42,74 minuten (gemiddelde snelheid 79,6 km/u).

Na de rit zwaaiden de coureurs en de pers de bouwkundig ingenieur, Franz Wallack, veel lof toe: de weg was „uitstekend aangelegd"... „volkomen veilig, ook voor de snelste ritten"...„ideaal"... „grote klasse"... „fantastisch"...en volgens de Britse Guardian een „uiterst belangwekkend stuk technische prestatie".

Ook vandaag profiteert de autoindustrie nog van dit „stuk technische prestatie". Sinds zijn opening in 1935 is de Großglockner-

route een klassieke testbaan voor het proberen van motoren en remmen. Als u dus per ongeluk een „langzaam" voertuig ontmoet, dat van allerlei.rare accessoires is voorzien, vreemde aanhangwagentjes meesleept en naar boven of naar beneden kruipt, dan kunt er zeker van zijn dat hier een autofirma bezig is de veiligheid van zijn produkten te perfectioneren.

's Zomers maken er ook heel wat wielrenners gebruik van deze col om hun conditie op de proef te stellen. Tevens is de „Glockner-etappe" sinds 1949 het hoogrepunt van de jaarlijkse „Österreich-Rundfahrt". De snelste tijd die ooit gereden is tussen het begin van de klim in Heiligenblut en de top van de pas (Hochtor) bedraagt 52,02 minuten, wat een gemiddelde snelheid van 16,1 kilometer betekent. En bijna elk jaar gaan de „slaven van de weg" nog sneller!

# Natuurbescherming en techniek

Al voordat begonnen was met de aanleg van de weg, die volgens Wallach „alle andere alpenwegen in de schadow zou moeten stellen", was er sprake van groeiende weerstand van natuurbeschermers tegen dit project. In 1918 had namelijk de Karintische industrieel Albrecht Wirth een gebied van bijna 41 vierkante kilometer rondom de Pasterze-gletscher gekocht en het aan de Alpenvereniging geschonken, met de verplichting dit alpine landschap „voor altijd als natuurbeschermingsgebied te behouden en het geen prooi te laten worden van speculanten uit de toeristenindustrie". Maar de Glocknerweg moest en zou tot de Franz-Jospehs-Höhe lopen, die aan de rand van dit natuurgebied ligt en een prachtig uitzicht biedt op de hoogste berg van Oostenrijk, de Großglockner, en op Oostenrijks gelijkmatigste gletscher, de Pasterze.

De natuurbeschermers hadden echter weinig kans tegen het belang van de werkgelegenheid. Gelukkig was Wallack niet alleen wegenbouwkundige, maar ook een uitstekende alpinist met veel gevoel voor de natuur. Vandaar dat hij bij de aanleg van de weg erg voorzichtig met het landschap omsprong: hij liet de begroeiing op het bouwtracé zorgvuldig verwijderen en de bomen en struiken opnieuw aanplanten in de berm van de weg en op andere plaatsen, die door de werkzaamheden ontsierd waren. Hij liet zelfs op verschillende hoogtes en in verschillende klimatologische zones plantentuinen aanleggen om gewassen te kweken, die hij dan later kon gebruiken ter verfraaiing en versterking van de bergweg.

Langs de hele Großglockner-route staan borden, die de toeristen aansporen op de natuur te passen. Natuurliefhebbers houden zich vanzelfsprekend aan zulke voorschriften, want de natuur, waarin, waarmee en waarvan wij allen leven wordt toch al genoeg belast door het gemotoriseerde verkeer.

# freytag & berndt

## Wanderkarten 1:50.000

GROSSGLOCKNER-HOCHALPENSTRASSEN AG

OFFIZIELLE KARTE 1:50.000

**Rund um die**

**Großglockner Hochalpenstraße**

**und Nationalpark**

**Hohe Tauern**

WK 121    Großvenediger–Oberpinzgau

WK 122    Großglockner–Kaprun–Zell am See

WK 123    Defereggen und Virgental

WK 382    Zell am See–Kaprun–Saalbach

WK 103    Pongau–Hochkönig–Saalfelden

WK 181    Kals–Heiligenblut–Matrei

WK 191    Gasteinertal–Wagrain–Großarltal

WK 193    Sonnblick–Großglocknerstraße–Unterpinzgau

**Erhältlich im Buch- und Zeitschriftenhandel**

Daardoor is het ook mogelijk dat de Großglocknerweg het nationale park Hoge Tauern tussen het Fuschertörl en het Hochtor en vanaf Guttal tot de Franz-Josefs-Höhe doorsnijdt zonder storend of ontsierend te werken.

Volgens de internationaal gerespecteerde professor in de architectuur Friedrich Achleitner voldoet deze bergroute ook aan de criteria van onze, wat dit betreft sensibel geworden tijd: „hoewel deze weg inderdaad nog een met handen vervaardigd produkt is, dat wil zeggen dat het terrein nog geen geweld kon worden aangedaan door het rigoreuze gebruik van machines, stond ook toen al voorop dat de ontsluitng van dit gebied niet ten koste mocht gaan van het landschappelijk schoon. Een bewijs voor het feit dat economische belangen en techniek een landschap niet perse hoeven te verwoesten.

## Eeuwenoude sporen

Deze weg over het Hochtor en door het kerngebied van het nationale park Hoge Tauern volgt oeroude sporen, die hun weerslag vinden in bijzonder interessante vondsten. In het „Beindlkar", ten zuiden van het Mittertörl werd bij kilometer 31 naast de weg een bronzen dolk uit de 17e eeuw voor Christus gevonden. Een stuk verder naar beneden ontdekte een houthakker een gedeelte van een Keltisch halsdiadeem uit de 5e eeuw voor Christus. Tijdens de aanleg van Hochtor stootten de arbeiders bij kilometer 33,4 op een beeld van Hercules uit de tijd van Augustus. Al deze vondsten bewijzen samen met andere vergelijkbare voorwerpen uit de beide dalen aan de voet van het Hochtor dat de Romeinen van deze Alpenpas gebruik hebben gemaakt. Ook in de middeleeuwen werd er via deze route levendig handel gedreven. Dat blijkt uit honderden hoefnagels, hoeven, sporen en allerlei beslagwerk, die langs deze weg te voorschijn zijn gekomen. En we kunnen in oude documenten lezen dat in die dagen ongeveer tien procent van het handelsverkeer tussen Venetië en Zuid-Duitsland en Bohemen over het Hochtor liep.

Voor de moderne automobilist is het bijna onvoorstelbaar dat de handel over de Alpen destijds hoofdzakelijk 's winters plaatsvond. Dat kwam omdat de meeste handelslieden 's zomers als boeren hun akkers moesten bestieren. Het feit dat er tijdens de winter handelsverkeer plaatsvond wordt duidelijk aan de hand van hoefnagels met doornen, die in grote getale langs de weg gevonden zijn - dat waren min of meer de voorlopers van onze autobanden met spikes. Op die manier had men in de winter meer „grip" op de weg.

Maar via het Hochtor verliepen ook minder vrolijke transporten. Bij het aanleggen van de zogenaamde „Hexenküche" (heksenkeuken) werden bij kilometer 23,5 boeien van gevangenen uit de 17e eeuw gevonden. In die tijd werden misdadigers en stropers in Salzburg namelijk nog al eens veroordeeld tot de „galeien", waarna ze aaneengeketend via het Hochtor naar Venetië werden gedreven.

Op verschillende plaatsen langs de Großglockner-route staan borden, die wijzen op de vroegere „Romeinse" weg die voor een groot gedeelte evenwijdig met de autoweg loopt. De overblijfselen van deze uitermate intelligent aangelegde weg, die twee tot vier meter breed is, dateren evenwel uit de middeleeuwen. Dat was de grote tijd van de transalpine handel met paard en wagen en van de goudmijnen in de Hoge Tauern.

De Romeinse schrijver Polybios (200-120 voor Chr.) beschrijft als volgt, wat in zijn tijd de mensen naar deze woeste bergstreek had gelokt: „op twee voet diepte zit goud, voor een deel zelfs degelijk goud ter grootte van bonen". En dat in zulke hoeveelheden dat „de goudprijs in Italië meteen met een derde daalde". In het midden van de 16e eeuw bereikte de gouddelving zijn grootste bloei met een jaarlijkse produktie van 870 kilo goud, voornamelijk in het gebergte ten oosten van de Großglockner-route, dat vandaag nog de Goldberggruppe (gouden bergen) heet. Dat was bijna tien procent van de goudproduktie in de toen bekende wereld. Salzburg werd daarom ook wel het „kleine Peru van de oude wereld" genoemd.

Het geoefende oog kan ook vandaag nog in de omgeving van het Hochtor de stortbergen van de middeleeuwse goudmijnen herkennen. En bij kilometer 32,6 duidt het bord „Knappenstube" (mijnwerkersvertrek) op een vervallen mijngang naast de Glocknerweg.

De grens tussen de Oostenrijkse provincies Karinthië en Salzburg loopt via het Hochtor. Deze natuurlijke grens over de belangrijkste Alpenketen brengt ook een interessant stuk geschiedenis aan het licht.

## Er trekken mensen de Alpen binnen

Toen de Bajuwaren zich in de 7e eeuw mondjesmaat in de noordelijke dalen van de Tauern vestigden moesten ze stukken oerwoud in weide- en akkerland veranderen. Namen als Hochmais aan de Glocknerweg (kilometer 21,6) of Maishofen wijzen duidelijk op het moeizaam rooien van bossen en het in cultuur brengen van land (oud-hoogduits meizan = rooien, kappen). Hetzelfde deden de Slaven, die wat later in het Mölltal gingen wonen. Dit blijkt uit de veldnaam Laserzen (laz = rooiing) en de dorpsnaam Stribach (strebsti = rooien). Voor de landbouw volkomen onbruikbaar en daarom niet meer dan een oriënteringspunt waren bijvoorbeeld het „Naßfeld"

*On the path from the Franz-Josefs-Höhe to the Oberwalder hut · Tussen de Franz-Josefs-Höhe en de Oberwalder-hut · En chemin de la Franz-Josefs-Höhe au refuge «Oberwalder-Hütte» · Lungo il cammino dalla Franz-Josefs-Höhe alla «Oberwalder-Hütte».*

(natte veld, moeras) bij kilometer 26 en het Messenaten (mizinat = moerassig) bij kilometer 35 ten zuiden van het Hochtor.

Het feit dat 1400 jaar geleden boeren en herders de Hoge Tauern in cultuur brachten is van groot historisch belang en vooral een prestatie om respect voor te hebben. De eerste geestelijken kwamen in de 12e en 13e eeuw in de Alpendorpjes te wonen. Zo bezit het Glocknerdorp Fusch een prachtige laat-romaanse kerktoren. En pas in de tijd van keizerin Maria Theresia (1740-1780) bereikte de schoolplicht deze afgelegen bergregionen. Nog een eeuw later vestigde de eerste arts zich in dit gebied.

Ongeveer twee eeuwen geleden kwamen er echter ook andere mensen naar de Hoge Tauern, die zich niet langer lieten afschrikken door verhalen over geesten, het weer brouwende heksen en fantastische monsters, die dit woeste, afgelegen gebied zouden bewonen. Anders dan voordien, toen slechts herders, jagers en een enkele botanicus op zoek naar geneeskrachtige kruiden naar boven durfden te gaan, begonnnen nu ook natuurwetenschappers zich te interesseren voor het hooggebergte. En dat was de eerste stap op weg naar het begaanbaar maken van de bergen en tevens het begin van het Alpinisme.

In 1799 organiseerde de Karintische vorst-bisschop Franz Xaver graaf Salm-Reifferscheid een expeditie van 30 personen en 13 paarden om de Großglockner te bedwingen. De onderneming mislukte door het slechte weer. Maar reeds in het jaar daarop slaagde een grote expeditie van 62 personen en 16 paarden er binnen twee dagen in de Adlersruhe (Adelaarsrust) te bereiken. Vandaar beklommen uiteindelijk vijf man de hoogste top van de Tauern, de Großglockner. Deze beide expedities werden door graaf Salm-Reifferscheid uit eigen zak betaald - en dat was een bedrag, waarvoor tegenwoordig 20 personen drie weken lang in grootse stijl door de Himalaja zouden kunnen trekken!

## Sneeuw en nog eens sneeuw

In de tolkantoren van de Großglockner-route verlangen vrouwen in de plaatselijke klederdracht helaas wat geld van de bezoekers. Op die manier hoeven onderhoud en verbetering van deze weg niet door de Oostenrijkse belastingbetaler gefinancierd te worden.

Juist een weg in het hooggebergte lijdt onder de niet te onderschatten verwoestende kracht van sneeuw en vorst, van lawines, aardverschuivingen en steenslag. Vandaar dat er heel wat financiële en technische middelen nodig zijn om het wegdek, de tunnels en de bruggen in stand te houden. Zo kunnen de gasten blijven genieten van een rit door een ruw landschap met een nog ruwer klimaat.

Tijdens de wintermaanden valt er gemiddeld vijf meter sneeuw op het hoogst gelegen gedeelte van de Großglockner-route (tussen 2300 en 2500 meter hoogte). Op zichzelf zou deze enorme hoeveelheid nog niet eens zo erg zijn. De wind, die hier vaak drie keer zo hard waait als in het dal – orkaankracht is geen zeldzaamheid – en het bovendien nooit laat afweten, is de ware boosdoener. Het komt dan ook vaak tot reusachtige sneeuwverstuivingen, zodat er zelfs 's zomers nog gigantische, overhangende sneeuwmassa's aan de uitstekende rotsen plakken.

Nu wordt ook begrijpelijk, waarom de Großglocknerweg op sommige plekken ook in juli omzoomd is door sneeuwhopen. Hier hebben de stormen 's winters echte sneeuwtorens laten ontstaan. In 1975 bereikten ze een recordhoogte van 21 meter – na het sneeuwvrij maken leek de weg meer op een ravijn tussen huizenhoge sneeuwbergen dan op een normale verkeersverbinding.

De technische vooruitgang heeft ook het sneeuwruimen veranderd. Tussen 1935 en 1937 schepten 350 man in gemiddeld 70 dagen 250.000 kubieke meter sneeuw weg om één rijbaan van de weg begaanbaar te maken. Vanaf 1953 nemen de door Wallach ontwikkelde rotatieploegen het werk over van ongeveer 1000 man. Sindsdien verwijderen vijf rotatieploegen en 30 man binnen 25 dagen 600.000 kubieke meter sneeuw van de hele weg, inclusief alle parkeerplaatsen. Het „sneeuwruimrecord" houdt het jaar 1975 met 800.000 kubieke meter sneeuw. Daarmee zou een goederentrein met een lengte van 250 km gevuld kunnen worden.

Het tolgeld wordt dus niet gebruikt om er een of ander burocratisch apparaat mee vol te proppen. Het is nodig om de bezoekers van de Großglockner-route een schitterende toeristische ervaring te kunnen blijven garanderen.

# De Pasterze

De bezoekers kunnen op de Franz-Josefs-Höhe iets beleven, wat nergens anders in Europa mogelijk is: een volkomen veilige en gemakkelijke wandeling over het blanke ijs van de 300 meter dikke Pasterze. Deze gletscher heeft een oppervlakte van 20 vierkante kilometer en een volume van van ongeveer twee kubieke kilometer. Vanaf de parkeerplaats Freiwandeck loopt sinds 1963 een kabelbaan naar de 143 meter hoger gelegen rand van de Pasterze. Met enige stappen bereikt u een door touwen afgegrensd stuk van dit glazig-blauwe ijsveld. Hier klateren reeds 's ochtends vroeg tientallen murmelende beekjes naar beneden. De toerist maakt hier een deel van de grote kringloop van het water mee: de zon laat de gletscher smelten en doet krachtig afbreuk aan zijn substantie. Maar slechts een paar kilometer hogerop ligt er op de Pasterze ook in de zomer sneeuw. Dat is het zogenaamde „voedingsgebied" van de gletscher. Onder 2800 meter hoogte begint dan het „verteergebied", het sneeuwvrije ijs, dat 's zomers langzaam wegsmelt.

Op een hoogte van ongeveer 3000 meter valt tweeënhalf keer

zoveel neerslag als in het dal en 90 procent van deze neerslag is sneeuw – dat zijn jaarlijks tussen zes en tien meter. Dit pak sneeuw krimpt onder invloed van warmte en het afwisselende ontdooien en bevriezen ineen tot een dikte van 20 tot 50 centimeter en verandert binnen circa 15 jaar in ijs.

De wetenschap ontraadselde pas twee eeuwen geleden het verband tussen het klimaat en het ontstaan van gletschers. Voor die tijd bedachten de godvrezende mensen allerlei andere verklaringen, die tegenwoordig als sages verder leven. Zo vertelt een legende dat er zich eens weelderige almweiden bevonden in het reusachtige trogdal, waarin de Pasterze ligt. Daar deden de Alpenbewoners zich tegoed aan losbandige braspartijen en dreven hun godslasterlijke driften op de spits door met kogels van boter op kegels uit kaas te mikken en de pastoor voor lege kerkbanken te laten prediken. Mateloos vertoornd liet God een verschrikkelijk onweer los, dat dit zondige dal volkomen overstroomde. Daarna liet Hij het vriezen dat het kraakte. Aldus verstarden de watermassa's en werden een stroom uit ijs, opdat deze poel van verderf voor altijd bedekt zou blijven en de mensen zouden leren waartoe goddeloosheid leidt.

## Een attractie voor miljoenen

Franz Wallack schatte in 1924 dat hij jaarlijks met 40.000 bezoekers van de Großglockner-route kon rekenen. Bij het begin van de aanleg van deze weg ging hij reeds uit van 120.000 bezoekers - en oogstte hiervoor honende kritiek van sceptische experts. Maar in 1938 - in het derde jaar na de voltooiing van de weg - werden er al bijna 98.000 voertuigen met 275.000 bezoekers geteld. Nu rijden er elk jaar gemiddeld 280.000 auto's over de Großglockner-route. Dat had reeds in de vijftiger jaren tot gevolg dat de weg verbreed moest worden om meer veiligheid en rijcomfort te bieden. De weg bezit sindsdien een breedte van minstens 7,5 meter (voordien zes meter) en op de moeilijkste stukken werd een derde rijstrook aangelegd. De radius van de bochten werd vergroot tot minstens 15 meter en het aantal parkeerplaatsen werd uitgebreid van 800 tot 4000.

Franz Wallack had zich eens ten doel gesteld om een weg over de Tauern aan te leggen, die een vergelijking met alle andere Alpenwegen kon doorstaan. Bijna 40 miljoen bezoekers hebben sindsdien bewezen dat Wallack zijn doel met de aanleg van deze fantastische route over de Alpen heeft bereikt.

---

*View from the summit of the Johannisberg onto the Pasterze · Blik vanaf de top van de Johannisberg op de Pasterze · Vue du sommet du Johannisberg sur la Pasterze · Veduta dalla cima del Johannisberg sulla Pasterze.*

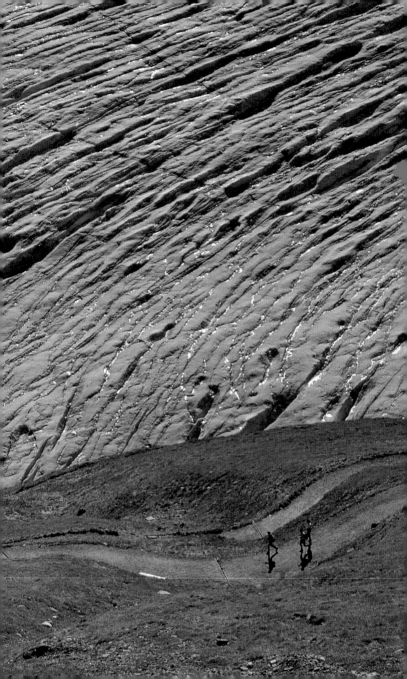

# Grandiose route des Alpes

«La venue de touristes aisés venant de pays lointains et désireux de visiter l'Autriche sans regarder à la dépense justifie la construction d'une route sur le Hochtor. Route qui, pour favoriser davantage le tourisme dans cette merveilleuse région, doit offrir un tracé intéressant, riche en vues grandioses et éclipser du point de vue technique toutes les autres routes de haute montagne connues jusqu'à présent».

C'est par de tels arguments qu'en 1924 un groupe d'hommes politiques et de fonctionnaires autrichiens étaya le projet hardi de construire la route alpine du Großglockner ; une étroite route de pierres de 3 mètres de large avec zones de dégagement visibles, conçue pour véhicules d'un poids allant jusqu'à 8 tonnes. Un millier d'ouvriers devait construire cette route sur le «Hochtor» au cours de deux étés.

Cependant, le manque de moyens financiers ne permit pas de réaliser ce projet. En effet, l'Autriche qui avait perdu la première guerre mondiale se trouva réduite au septième de sa grandeur impériale et de sa puissance économique. Mais cette situation ainsi que l'inflation catastrophique n'empêchèrent pas les autorités de charger Franz Wallack, jeune ingénieur de Carinthie, d'élaborer ce projet de la route alpine du Großglockner.

Quatre années après cette décision, Franz Rehrl, Gouverneur du Land de Salzbourg, eut, fin 1928, l'idée d'adopter le gigantesque

40/41 ◀ *Gamsgrubenweg with view of the Pasterze (left) and the Johannisberg · Gamsgrubenpad met blik op de Pasterze (links) en de Johannisberg · Gamsgrubenweg avec vue sur la Pasterze (à gauche) et le Johannisberg · Il Gamsgrubenweg con veduta sulla Pasterze (sinistra) e sul Johannisberg.*

projet de la société berlinoise AEG de construire une centrale hydro-électrique dans les montagnes des Hohe Tauern et de profiter de la route nécessaire pour le chantier en l'améliorant par la suite pour en faire la route alpine du Großglockner tant rêvée, après avoir indemnisé la société. Malheureusement, la nature fit échouer ce projet, car avec chaque averse le canal d'essai installé sur le versant se bouchait désespérément.

## L' idée prend forme

La centrale hydro-électrique de l'AEG qui aurait dû donner naissance à la route du Großglockner fut donc abandonnée. Il est presque grotesque de constater que ce fut la crise économique qui relança le projet. Car, en octobre 1929, l'écroulement de la bourse de New York, déclenchant une crise mondiale, provoqua des répercussions catastrophiques sur l'Autriche déjà secouée par de graves crises internes. Le pays se vit contraint de décider en 1930 la construction de la route alpine sur le Großglockner pour adoucir les effets de la crise et aussi la situation desespérée sur le marché du travail et dans le secteur du bâtiment.

L'ampleur de la terrible crise économique sur la population est illustrée par quelques données. De 1929 à 1933, le nombre de chômeurs enregistrés passa de 200.000 à 557.000, ce qui représente une augmentation de 26 pour cent. Le produit national brut baissa, en même temps, de 11,3 milliards à 8,8 milliards de schillings ; 16.400 entreprises firent faillite et la consommation diminua d'un cinquième; par exemple, la production de bière baissa de 5,2 à 3,1 millions d'hectolitres. Ce n'est qu'en ayant ce désolant tableau devant les yeux que la construction de la route du Großglockner de 1939 à 1935 prend toute son importance du point de

vue politique de l'emploi. Pendant 26 mois, la construction de la route fit vivre 3200 personnes en moyenne.

Le 30 août 1930, des vedettes de la politique, des stratèges du tourisme, une douzaine de journalistes et une foule de curieux se rassemblèrent pour être témoins de l'extraordinaire coup d'envoi des travaux, ponctué par des centaines de détonations tout le long du tracé jalonné. Ce fut un événement qui eut un écho retentissant même dans la presse internationale.

Contrairement à la variante «bon marché» proposée en 1924 (route de pierres de 3 mètres de large avec zones de dégagement), on se mit alors à la construction d'une route de montagne large de 6 mètres «pour la grande circulation», qui devait rejeter dans l'ombre toutes les célèbres routes alpines du point de vue technique.

Car même la crise n'avait pu freiner le développement rapide de la circulation routière. De 1924 à 1930, le nombre d'automobilistes en Autriche avait doublé pour atteindre 17.350 (en 1986, on en comptait 2,6 millions). En Allemagne, ce même chiffre avait presque triplé pour atteindre 650.000. D'ailleurs, les Allemands représentaient en 1930 environ 53% des 1,8 millions de touristes étrangers en Autriche.

La construction de la route alpine du Großglockner permet également d'avoir un aperçu impressionnant sur la situation sociale à cette époque. Les salaires de base pour une semaine de 48 heures de travail se situaient entre 52 schillings (ouvrier qualifié) et 75 schillings (contremaître). Le kilo de pain noir coûtait 58 groschens, la viande de boeuf 3,60 schillings et le beurre 6 schillings. Une cigarette valait 3 groschens, un petit pain 7, un oeuf 14, un demi litre de

*An ibex near the Freiwandeck parking area · Een steenbok in de buurt van het parkeerterrein Freiwandeck · Bouquetin près du parking Freiwandeck · Uno stambecco nelle vicinanze del parcheggio Freiwandeck.*

bière 48 et un kilowattheure d'électricité 70. Pour un litre d'essence super, il fallait dépenser 1 schilling.

A titre de comparaison, voici quelques traitements mensuels de cette époque: Le Président de la République fédérale touchait par mois 3913 schillings, un professeur de lycée de l'échelon le plus élevé 730 schillings et un fonctionnaire d'état commençait avec un salaire de base de 137 schillings. Le Président de la République aurait dû dépenser presque deux mois de traitement pour l'achat d'une voiture demi-luxe comme la très populaire «Steyr 100» qui était une voiture avec moteur quatre cylindres, cylindrée de 1,2 litres, 32 chevaux et qui atteignait une vitesse maximale de 100 km/heure avec une consommation d'essence de 9 à 10,5 litres. Même la plus petite voiture valait la somme fabuleuse de 5.000 schillings, ce qui se comprend très bien vu le nombre très limité de voitures sortant de l'usine.

## In te domine speravi

Le soir du 2 août 1935, un feu gigantesque sur l'Edelweißspitze (2571 m) annonça l'achèvement de la route alpine du Großglockner. L'information distribuée à la presse à l'occasion de l'ouverture le 3 août donnait des chiffres impressionnants:

La route du Großglockner mesure 6 mètres de large et 58,5 km de long. Elle remonte d'abord le Fuscher Tal de Bruck à Heiligenblut (48 km); puis, le deuxième tronçon de 1,8 km conduit du Fuschertörl sur l'Edelweißspitze, en offrant un superbe panorama ; et, les 8,7 km de la «route des glaciers« relient Guttal et le plateau Franz-Josefs-Höhe. 33,4 hectares furent transformés en routes et parkings; 67 pont s, 2 tunnels (Hochtor 311 mètres et Mittertörl 117 mètres) furent construits; on installa 48 km de câbles téléphoniques et 24 postes téléphones-secours et on aménagea 18 parkings dans des endroits pittoresques.

Le coût de construction de cet ouvrage s'éleva à 25,8 millions de schillings, c'est à dire 200.000 schillings de moins que prévus et ceci correspond à 5% des investissements autrichiens en 1935. Cette somme paraît raisonnable quand on sait que le pont sur le Danube construit aussi à Vienne au milieu des années trente (il s'agit du «Reichsbrücke» qui s'écroula en 1976) a coûté 24 millions de schillings.

Hélas, la construction et l'entretien de cette route alpine coûtèrent la vie à 20 personnes. La chapelle commémorative au Fuschertörl fut construite d'après des plans de Clemens Holzmeister.

*The Großglockner is the greatest attraction of the Hohe Tauern National Park · De Großglockner is het pronkstuk van het nationale park Hoge Tauern · Le Großglockner est le joyau du Parc National Hohe Tauern · Il Großglockner è l'attrazione del parco nazionale degli Alti Tauri.*

Lorsque les ouvriers creusèrent le tunnel du Hochtor en l'été 1933, ils trouvèrent une pièce d'argent datant de l'époque de l'Impératrice Marie-Thérèse avec l'inscription «In te domine speravi» (O Seigneur, c'est en toi que je mets mon espérance). Wallack grava cette phrase sur l'entrée du «Hochtor» en signe de remerciement pour la réussite de cet ouvrage en dépit de tous les obstacles. Cette inscription reflète la confiance en Dieu lors des périodes extrêmement dures.

La première épreuve sportive empruntant la route alpine du Großglockner eut lieu dès le 4 août 1935, le lendemain de l'inauguration: 75 coureurs automobiles participèrent à la «Première Course Internationale du Großglockner» sur une distance de 19,5 km et avec une différence d'altitude de 1600 mètres jusqu'au Fuschertörl. L'Italien Mario Tadini sur Alfa Romeo (catégorie de voitures de course de plus de 2000 cm$^3$) remporta la victoire sur cette route non encore asphaltée (ce n'est qu'en 1939 que toute la route fut revêtue d'une couche d'asphalte). Il mit 14:42,74 minutes; soit une moyenne de 79,6 km/h.

Après la compétition, les coureurs et la presse chantèrent les louanges du constructeur Wallack «La route est tracée à merveille... tout-à-fait sûre même pour de grandes vitesses... construite de façon idéale et excellente...une route superbe» et le journal britannique «Guardian» parle d'une performance technique très significative».

L'industrie automobile ne cesse d'en tirer partie, car la route alpine du Großglockner est, depuis qu'elle existe, la piste d'essai classique pour tester les moteurs et les freins. Si vous rencontrez donc de temps en temps des véhicules «lents» dotés d'équipements étranges ou de remorques bizarres, avec des feux clignotants, vous pouvez être sûrs qu'il s'agit d'une société automobile en train de se creuser la tête pour savoir comment perfectionner la sécurité technique d'une voiture.

En été, l'automobiliste rencontre des cyclistes qui s'efforcent de vaincre cette route alpine. L'étape du Großglockner par le Hochtor est d'ailleurs chaque année le point culminant du tour d'Autriche. Le record pour la montée au Hochtor (52,02 minutes) avec une moyenne de 16,1 kilomètres par heure permet d'apprécier la performance de ces «géants de la route».

## Protection de la nature et technique

Bien avant le commencement des travaux, ce projet ambitieux fut l'objet d'une résistance de plus en plus forte de la part des défenseurs de la nature. En effet, en 1918, Albrecht Wirth, industriel de Carinthie dans le secteur du bois, avait acquis une superficie de presque 41 kilomètres carrés autour du glacier «Pasterze» et avait offert ce territoire au Club Alpin à condition qu'il préservât à jamais ce site des hautes alpes contre l'industrie touristique spéculative et qu'il le conservât comme parc national. Cependant, la route du Großglockner devait arriver jusqu'au plateau «Franz-Josefs-Höhe», un endroit qui avoisine ce parc national et qui offre une vue incomparable sur le plus beau glacier et sur la plus haute montagne d'Autriche.

Mais les considérations d'ordre économique l'emportèrent sur les revendications écologistes. Wallack était heureusement non seulement constructeur de routes, mais aussi excellent alpiniste, et il était doté d'un sens aigu pour tout ce qui avait trait à la protection de la nature. Il a donc, durant la construction, donné la priorité à la protection des sites. Il exigea que la végétation du tracé soit enlevée prudemment pour couvrir ensuite talus et autres cicatrices causées par les travaux. Wallack fit même aménager des jardins dans différentes zones selon l'altitude et les conditions climatiques afin d'y cultiver des plantes adaptées au climat pouvant servir plus tard lors de l'agrandissement et de la modernisation de cette route.

*Suite page 51*

## Tauernautobahn: Road through Nature

The Tauern Motorway has earned this name which leads from Salzburg through the main Alpine ridge to Villach and, in its most impressive portion, even has access from the east to the Hohe Tau-

ern National Park. Here – in the area of Katschberg and the Radstädter Tauern range – the Romans over 2000 years ago had already built a comparatively comfortable and fast detour from upper Italy and past the high mountains to the east, to the north into the Danube plain.

The storms of mass migration literally obliterated this Roman Tauern Highway. It took until around 1520 before the Salzburg archbishops again laid down a roadway on the Roman foundation through the Radstädter Tauern range and Katschberg, in order to facilitate the increasing traffic between Germany and the world trade center, Venice.

Today, this "road through nature" follows those ancient tracks from which the access roads in Bischofshofen and in Spittal branch off to the Großglockner Alpine Highway.

## Tauernautobahn: Weg door het groen

De Tauernautosnelweg, die van Salzburg dwars door de Alpen naar Villach loopt, is een weg midden door de natuur en bovendien een indrukwekkende toegangsweg tot het oostelijke deel van het nationale park Hoge Tauern. Hier – in het gebied van de Katschberg en de Radstädter Tauern – legden de Romeinen reeds meer dan 2000 jaar geleden een relatief gerieflijke en snelle bergweg aan, die Noord-Italië langs de oostkant van de Alpen met de Donauvlakte verbond.

De daarop volgende donkere eeuwen der Volksverhuizingen hebben deze Romeinse Alpenweg letterlijk tot stof doen vergaan. Het duurde tot 1520, voordat de Salzburgse aartsbischoppen weer een begaanbare weg lieten aanleggen over de Radstädter Tauern en de Katschberg, waarbij ze gebruik maakten van de Romeinse fundamenten. Op die manier kon de groeiende verkeerstroom tussen een van de centra van de wereldhandel, Venetië, en Duitsland in betere banen worden geleid.

Vandaag volgt de Tauernautosnelweg, de „weg door het groen", deze oeroude sporen. In Bischofshofen en Spittal kunnen de toeristen van deze snelweg afslaan, om de Großglockner-route te bereiken.

## Tauernautobahn: La strada nel verde

L'autostrada dei Tauri merita questo nome. Parta da Salisburgo a Villach attraverso la cresta montuosa principale delle Alpi e, nel suo tratto più imponente, tocca anche da oriente il parco nazionale degli Alti Tauri. Qui, nella zona di Katschberg e Radstädter Tauern, già i Romani costruirono più di 2.000 anni fa una strada più lunga comoda e rapida dall'Italia settentrionale lungo la parte orientale delle alte Alpi fino a nord nella pianura del Danubio.

Le bufere della migrazione di popoli hanno letteralmente spazzato

via questa strada romana dei Tauri. Durò fino al 1520 circa prima che gli arcivescovi di Salisburgo fecero nuovamente costruire una strada sul fondamento romano lungo il Radstädter Tauern e il Katschberg. Ciò favorì il commercio fra la Germania e il centro commerciale mondiale di Venezia.

La «strada nel verde» segue oggi queste antichissime tracce; da essa gli svincoli di Bischofshofen e di Spittal portano alla strada alpina del Großglockner.

---

*Suite de la page 49*

Plusieurs écriteaux le long de la route alpine prient les touristes de protéger l'environnement, ce qui est évident pour les amis de la nature, car un tourisme intense constitue une contrainte pour la nature – dans laquelle, par laquelle et avec laquelle nous vivons tous.

Tout cela explique pourquoi la route alpine s'intègre bien dans le parc national «Hohe Tauern» qu'elle traverse entre le Fuscher Törl et le Hochtor d'une part et entre Guttal et le plateau Franz-Josefs-Höhe d'autre part.

Ainsi, la construction et le tracé de cette route alpine respectent même les critères de notre époque aux dires du grand professeur autrichien d'architecture Friedrich Hochleitner. «Comme cette route fut construite de manière artisanale, même l'utilisation de machines ne put détruire ce magnifique paysage. C'est la preuve que les intérêts économiques et l'esprit technique ne doivent pas forcément défigurer l'environnement».

# Des traces millénaires

La découverte d'impressionnantes trouvailles montre que cette route sur le Hochtor, qui traverse le parc national «Hohe Tauern», suit des traces très anciennes.

Dans le «Beindlkar» au sud du tunnel du Mittertörl (au kilomètre 31), on trouva un poignard en bronze datant du 17ème siècle avant Jésus Christ. Environ à deux heures de marche de cet endroit, un bûcheron trouva un morceau d'un collier celtique du 5ème siècle avant Jésus Christ. Lors de la construction du Hochtor (au kilomètre 33,4), d'autres vestiges furent découverts par les ouvriers, comme la statuette d'Hercule et des morceaux d'une lampe romaine en argile qui remontent à l'époque de la naissance de Jésus Christ. Ceci prouve que les Romains ont dû utiliser ce col alpin, puisque des trouvailles similaires furent découvertes dans les vallées des deux côtés du Hochtor. Les centaines de clous à ferrer, de fers, d'éperons et de ferrures de bride trouvés le long du tracé de la route, témoignent également d'un commerce florissant au Moyen Age empruntant ce col. De vieux documents relatent d'ailleurs qu'à cette époque 10% environ du trafic de marchandises entre Venise, qui était un centre florissant, et la région de l'Allemagne du Sud et la Bohème, passaient par une route sur le Hochtor.

L'automobiliste de nos jours ne peut s'imaginer que le trafic transalpin en ce temps avait surtout lieu en hiver, car la majorité des commerçants était des paysans, obligés de labourer la terre en été. Les clous à ferrer garnis d'épines trouvés en grande quantité le long de la route témoignent de ce commerce exercé en hiver - ils sont en quelque sorte les précurseurs de nos pneus à clous en hiver.

Mais de tristes transports empruntèrent également cette route vers le Sud en passant par le Hochtor. Lors de l'élargissement du tronçon de la «Hexenküche» (Cuisine des sorcières, au kilomètre 23,5), on découvrit des chaînes de prisonniers du 17ème siècle. A l'époque, on enchaînait souvent les criminels et les braconniers de Salzbourg et on les envoyait aux galères à Venise par la route du Hochtor.

A plusieurs endroits le long de la route alpine du Großglockner, des écriteaux attirent l'attention sur la «Route des Romains», parallèle à la nouvelle route sur des distances importantes. Ce qui reste de cette route de 4 mètres de large, tracée de façon extrêmement intelligente, remonte toutefois au Moyen Age, à l'époque brillante de l'extraction de l'or dans les Hohe Tauern et du commerce transalpin qui se faisait à dos de cheval.

L'écrivain romain Polybios (environ 200 - 120 avant J.-C.) rapporta, en décrivant ce qui attirait déjà les hommes à son époque dans cette contrée sauvage des Alpes, que «l'or extrait en grande quantité et en véritables pépites parfois, à des profondeurs de deux

*Road construction in 1932 in steep terrain in the high mountains · Wegenbouw in de Alpen in 1932 · Construction de la route en 1932 en terrain abrupt · La costruzione stradale del 1932 sul ripido terreno delle alte Alpi.*

pieds, a fait chuter les cours de ce métal d'un tiers en Italie». L'extraction de l'or atteignit son apogée vers le milieu du 16ème siècle, époque à laquelle la production annuelle s'éleva à 870 kilos environ et il provenait pour la majeure partie des mines à l'Est de la route du Großglockner. Ces montagnes portent encore aujourd'hui le nom «Goldberggruppe» (Groupe des montagnes de l'or). A l'époque, environ 10% de la production mondiale de l'or provenaient de Salzbourg, nommé aussi le «Petit Pérou de l'ancien continent».

L' oeil avisé peut encore maintenant découvrir, dans les environs du Hochtor, les terrils des mines du Moyen Age. L'écriteau «Knappenstube» au kilomètre 32,6 indique l'entrée effondrée d'une galerie à côté de la route du Großglockner.

Le Hochtor marque la frontière entre le Land de Salzbourg et la Carinthie. Cette frontière naturelle constituée par la crête principale des Alpes représente aussi un chapitre remarquable de l'histoire.

## Les hommes peuplent les Alpes

Lorsqu'au 7ème siècle, les Bavarois colonisèrent les vallées au Nord des Tauern, ils durent déboiser les forêts et les remplacer par d'autres cultures. Des noms comme «Hochmais» (au kilomètre 21,6) sur la route du Glockner ou «Maishofen» nous renseignent clairement sur le défrichement laborieux qu'ils durent entreprendre (en vieil allemand «meizan» veut dire «défricher»). Il en est de même pour les Slaves qui, à l'époque, s'installèrent dans la vallée de la Möll; c'est ce qu'indique le lieu-dit «Laserzen» («laz» = défrichement) ou «Stribach» («strebsti» = défrichement). Par contre, le Nassfeld sur le flanc nord de la route alpine du Großglockner (au kilomètre 26) et aussi le «Mesenaten» (au kilomètre 35) au Sud du Hochtor sont des régions marécageuses qui n'ont absolument pas de valeur agricole et servent seulement de point d'orientation («mizinat» = marécageux, même sens que «Naßfeld»).

La dimension historique qui s'ouvre devant nous ne peut que forcer notre respect. Il y a environ 1400 ans, des paysans et des bergers cultivèrent les «Hohe Tauern». Le clocher impressionnant du village de Fusch est de style roman tardif et permet de conclure que des prêtres s'établirent dans les villages alpins au 12ème ou au 13ème siècle. Ce n'est qu'à l'époque de l'Impératrice Marie-Thérèse (1740-1780) que l'enseignement scolaire devenu obligatoire s'imposa dans les vallées des Alpes. Un siècle plus tard, le premier médecin vint s'installer dans cette région.

*54/55 ♦ A sunny day along the Fuschertörl after a night's snow fall · Na een sneeuwrijke nacht schijnt de zon boven het Fuschertörl · Après une chute de neige nocturne, journée ensoleillée sur le Fuschertörl · Giornata di sole sul Fuschertörl dopo una notte di neve.*

Ce n'est qu'il y a deux siècles environ que des gens venus dans les Hohe Tauern réalisèrent que cette contrée vierge n'était pas seulement la demeure de fantômes, de monstres épouvantables et de sorcières capables de provoquer des orages. Jadis, seuls les chasseurs et les bergers osaient s'aventurer sur ces hauteurs et parfois

*Technical equipment for road construction in 1934 · Technische uitrusting bij de aanleg van de weg in 1934 · Equipements utilisés lors de la construction de la route en 1934 · Equipaggiamento tecnico per la costruzione stradale del 1934.*

des botanistes y pénétraient à la recherche d'herbes médicinales. Des scientifiques commencèrent aussi à s'intéresser à cette montagne, ce qui donna l'impulsion nécessaire pour la mise en valeur des Alpes et le développement de l'alpinisme.

En 1799, le comte Franz Xaver Salm-Reifferscheid, prince- évêque de Carinthie, équipa une expédition de 30 personnes et 13 chevaux pour partir à la conquête du Großglockner. Le mauvais temps fit échouer la tentative. Mais un an plus tard, une grande expédition de 62 personnes et 16 chevaux réussit à avancer jusqu'à l'Adlers-ruhe en deux jours, d'où cinq hommes purent finalement atteindre le point culminant des Tauern. Le comte Salm-Reifferscheid avait financé les deux expéditions de sa propre poche. Il dépensa une somme qui permettrait aujourd'hui de financer une expédition de 3 semaines pour 20 personnes dans l'Himalaya.

## Imposantes masses de neige

Des employées en beaux costumes régionaux doivent malheureu-sement percevoir un péage, car l'entretien et l'aménagement de cette route nécessitent des sommes qui ne doivent pas être à la charge des contribuables.

Les dégâts causés par la neige, le gel, les avalanches, les glisse-ments de terrain ou les chutes de pierres occasionnent des dépen-ses très élevées du point de vue technique et financier. Le revête-ment de la chaussée exige un entretien permanent pour assurer aux usagers une traversée sans problèmes dans un terrain extrêmement exposé aux caprices de la nature.

Pendant l'hiver, il tombe environ 5 mètres de neige sur le sommet de la route alpine du Großglockner (entre 2300 et 2500 mètres d'al-titude). Il faut noter qu'à une telle altitude il y a toujours du vent qui souffle à des vitesses qui atteignent jusqu'à 130 kmh, c'est-à-dire

**Salzburger Automobil-, Motorrad- und Touring-Club**
Your Partner in the Mountains
Uw partner in het gebergte
Votre partenaire en montagne
Il suo socio in montagna

trois fois la vitesse moyenne dans la vallée. Ceci explique les immenses déplacements de neige et la formation de gigantesques amas que l'on peut encore remarquer en été sur les arêtes.

C'est la raison pour laquelle il y a encore au mois de juillet de la neige sur les bas-côtés de certains tronçons de la route. En hiver, les tempêtes de neige assez fréquentes couvrent la route d'une couche plus ou moins grande. En 1975, on enregistra un record, car la hauteur de neige dégagée sur les deux bords de la route atteignit 21 mètres. Ceci correspond à une rue bordée de hauts immeubles dans une grande ville.

Le progrès technique se reflète aussi dans les méthodes de déneigement. Entre 1935 et 1937, 350 hommes débarassaient 250.000 m$^3$ de neige en 70 jours en moyenne, pour dégager une seule voie. Depuis 1953, les chasse-neige à rotation spécialement conçus par Wallack font théoriquement le travail d'environ 1000 personnes avec une pelle. Cinq chasse-neige et 30 personnes dégagent la route et les parkings de 600.000 m$^3$ de neige et ceci en 25 jours. Le record appartient à l'année 1975 avec 800.000 m$^3$ de neige débarassée. Ceci aurait suffi pour remplir un convoi de 250 km de long.

Les revenus du péage ne sont donc pas destinés à financer un important service administratif, mais ils assurent la mise en oeuvre des techniques les plus modernes dans le but d'offrir aux usagers un souvenir extraordinaire.

## Le glacier de la Pasterze

Les visiteurs de la Franz-Josefs-Höhe ne doivent pas manquer une aventure unique en Europe : la promenade sans risques et sans efforts sur le glacier de la Pasterze d'une superficie d'environ 20 km$^2$ et d'un volume de 2 km$^3$, dont l'épaisseur peut atteindre jusqu'à 300 mètres. Depuis 1963, un funiculaire descend du parking «Freiwandeck» jusqu'au glacier situé à 143 mètres plus bas. A quelques pas du funiculaire, les touristes peuvent commencer leur promenade dans la zone délimitée par des cordes sur le glacier éblouissant. Vers midi déjà, on entend le bruit de nombreux petits cours d'eau, ce qui fait découvrir au visiteur le cycle de l'eau. Le soleil fait fondre une partie du glacier et diminue ainsi sa substance. Par contre, à quelques kilomètres plus haut subsiste sur le glacier, même en été, une couche de neige qui «nourrit le glacier». La limite entre les deux zones se situe à environ 2800 mètres d'altitude.

Au-dessus de 3000 mètres d'altitude, on enregistre deux fois et

*The curves of the Zlamitzen cling to the terrain · De haarspeldboch-▶ 60/61
ten van Zlamitzen passen zich soepel aan het landschap aan · Les
lacets des Zlamitzen épousent le terrain · Le curve della Zlamitzen
si adattano al terreno.*

demie plus de précipitations que dans les vallées, dont 90 % sous forme de neige, soit entre 6 et 10 m par an. Sous l'influence de la chaleur et du cycle fonte-gel, la masse de neige diminue pour atteindre une épaisseur de 20 à 50 cm et se transforme en glace en une période de 15 années environ.

Ce n'est qu'il y a un peu plus de deux siècles seulement que la science trouva une explication aux rapports entre le climat et la formation d'un glacier. Auparavant les gens qui craignaient Dieu avaient recours à des explications qui continuent à exister dans des mythes.

D'après la légende, il y avait jadis, à l'endroit où le glacier de la Pasterze remplit actuellement un gigantesque bassin, d'abondants alpages où les habitants s'adonnaient à une vie de débauche et insultaient la religion en jouant aux quilles de fromage avec des boules de beurre, tandis que le curé prêchait dans une église déserte. La légende raconte encore que Dieu se fâcha et envoya un formidable orage qui balaya cette vie de péché. Ensuite, Dieu envoya un froid glacial qui transforma les eaux en une coulée de glace pour que les lieux de la débauche soient à jamais ensevelis et que tous les êtres humains sachent que l'impiété engendre un châtiment exemplaire.

## Une attraction pour des millions de visiteurs

En 1924, Wallack estima qu'environ 40.000 visiteurs viendraient visiter chaque année la route alpine du Großglockner. Au commencement des travaux en 1930, Wallack avança le chiffre de 120.000 visiteurs et devint la cible de critiques ironiques de la part des experts. Cependant, en 1938, la troisième année après l'inauguration, on comptait déjà 98.000 véhicules avec 275.000 visiteurs. De nos jours, 280.000 véhicules passent en moyenne par la route alpine du Großglockner. Il fallut donc élargir la route, ce qui fut fait au début des années cinquante, afin de pouvoir faire face aux exigences de sécurité et de confort. La route fut élargie de 6 à 7,5 mètres au moins et dotée de trois voies sur les tronçons les plus difficiles. En outre, les rayons des virages furent agrandis de 10 à 15 mètres au moins et le nombre de places de parking fut porté de 800 à 4000.

Franz Wallack s'était fixé pour but de construire une route sur les Hohe Tauern éclipsant par sa perfection toutes les autres routes alpines. Wallack a gagné son pari et les 40 millions de visiteurs qui sont venus jusqu'à présent admirer cette oeuvre gigantesque sont la preuve éclatante de la réussite de cette superbe route des Alpes.

*The curves of the Glockner Highway are a special thrill for motorcyclists · De scherpe bochten van de Glockner-route vormen een bijzondere uitdaging voor motorrijders · Les lacets de la route du Großglockner représentent un attrait particulier pour les motards · Le curve della strada del Glockner sono un'attrazione notevole per i motociclisti.*

# La meravigliosa strada delle Alpi

«Per la costruzione di una strada artificiale sul Hochtor è decisivo l'efficiente turismo internazionale di tali stranieri in grado di spendere molto denaro in Austria. Per incrementare il turismo è necessaria una strada guidata in modo interessante e ricca d'immagini che metta in ombra, tecnicamente,tutte le famose strade alpine».

*The Italian, Mario Tadini, won the first Glockner race in 1935 · De Italiaan Mario Tadini won in 1935 de eerste Glockner-race · L'Italien Mario Tadini remporta en 1935 la première course du Großglockner · L'italiano Mario Tadini fu il vincitore della prima Corsa del Glockner nel 1935.*

Con tali argomenti pretenziosi un gruppo di politici e funzionari austriaci consolidò, nel 1924, l'audace piano di costruire la strada alpina del Großglockner: una stradina massicciata di tre metri di larghezza, facendo largo a vista, per veicoli fino ad otto tonnellate di peso. 1000 operai avrebbero costruito questa strada in due estati.

Gli autorevoli signori progettarono però un castello in aria poiché mancava il denaro. Avendo perso nella I. guerra mondiale, l'Austria si era ridotta ad un settimo della sua grandezza imperiale e della sua forza economica. Soffriva di un'inflazione catastrofale. Tuttavia, il giovane ingegnere carinziano Franz Wallack, ottenne l'incarico di costruire la strada del Glockner.

Passarono quattro anni, finché, alla fine del 1928, il presidente della regione Salisburgo, Franz Rehrl, concepì un'idea liberatrice: utilizzare l'energia idraulica degli Alti Tauri sarebbe stata la soluzione. Un enorme progetto della AEG berlinese presupponeva una strada per la costruzione sul Hochtor. Si sarebbe potuto, in seguito, mutare il fine di questa strada e prepararla per farla diventare la strada alpina del Großglockner. Questo progetto però fallì a causa della natura, poiché ogni acquazzone otturava irrimediabilmente il canale con detriti.

## Prende forma un'idea

Fu squalificato di conseguenza l'AEG «Tauernwerk» come assistente per la nascita della strada del Großglockner. Coprì questo ruolo, in modo grottesco, la grande crisi economica che si riversò sul mondo dopo il tracollo della borsa di New York nell'ottobre del 1929. La crisi portò l'Austria, già minata da gravi crisi politiche interne, verso una disastrosa discesa. Ciò forzò infine, nel 1930, la decisione di costruire la strada alpina del Großglockner per attenuare in tale modo gli effetti della catastrofe sul mercato e sull'economia edilizia.

L'effetto terribilmente duro della crisi economica sulla popolazione

*Segue a pagina 68*

---

# To the Sunny Side of the Glockner · Naar de zonnige kant van de Glockner · La parte assolata del Glockner

After an excursion across the Hochtor to the South, the road through the Felbertauern range offers itself as a return route, especially for a short detour in the idyllic mountain climber village of Kals on the sunny side of the Großglockner. From here, the "Kalser Glockner Highway" leads to the Luckner cabin at 2000 m. above sea level, the most favourable departure point for climbing the Großglockner.

Kals still remains a typical Tyrolian mountain farm village whose hospitality and charm have been praised by its touristic explorers for over a century.

---

Na een uitstapje via het Hochtor naar het zuiden is het een goed idee om over de Felbertauern-route terug te rijden – vooral omdat zo een kort bezoek kan worden gebracht aan het idyllische bergbeklimmersdorpje Kals, dat aan de zonzijde van de Großglockner ligt. Vandaar loopt de „Kal-

ser Glocknerweg" naar het Lucknerhuis op 2000 m hoogte, het beste uitgangspunt voor een beklimming van de Großglockner.

Kals is tot de huidige dag een typisch Tirools boerendorpje gebleven, dat al meer dan een eeuw geleden bij zijn toeristische ontdekkers bekend stond voor zijn gastvrijheid en charme.

La strada attraverso il Felbertauern si presenta come via del ritorno dopo un'escursione attraverso il Hochtor fino a sud. Vale la pena, prima di tutto, per una breve scappata nell'idilliaco villaggio di alpinisti Kals, sulla parte soleggiata del Großglockner. La «Kalser Glocknerstraße» porta di lì al Lucknerhaus, a 2.000 m sul livello del mare, al miglior punto di partenza per la scalata del Großglockner.

Kals è rimasto fin'oggi quel tipico villaggio di contadini tirolesi della cui ospitalità e fascino già parlarono i suoi scopritori turistici più di un secolo fa.

**Information and brochures / Inlichtingen en foldermateriaal / Informazioni e prospetti: Verkehrsbüro (Tourist Office / VVV / Ufficio per il turismo) 9981 Kals am Großglockner, Tel. 04876/211.**

*Segue da pagina 65*

è illustrato da alcuni dati: dal 1929 al 1933 il numero dei «disoccupati registrati» salì da scarsi 2oo.ooo a 557.000, ovvero il 26%. Il prodotto nazionale lordo diminuì da 11,3 miliardi a 8,8 miliardi di scellini, 16.400 ditte fallirono ed il consumo diminuì di un quinto - quello della birra ad esempio, da 5,2 a 3,1 milioni di ettolitri. La costruzione della strada alpina del Großglockner ottiene, di fronte a quest'opprimente scenario, la sua importanza di impiego politico dal 1930 al 1935: in media 3.200 persone trovarono il loro pane con la costruzione della strada per 26 mesi.

Il 30 agosto del 1930 si riunirono a Ferleiten i notabili politici, strateghi del turismo, dozzine di giornalisti ed una marea di curiosi per assistere alla straordinaria drammaturgia della prima esplosione: furono fatte esplodere centinaia di cariche esplosive in serie lungo il tracciato fissato, il cui rimbombo ebbe un'eco notevole addirittura nella stampa internazionale.

Rispetto alla «variante a buon mercato» progettata nel 1924 (stradina massicciata di tre metri di larghezza) ci si avviò ora, dopo i discorsi ufficiali pieni di speranza, verso la costruzione di una strada alpina di sei metri di larghezza «per il grande traffico», la quale avrebbe dovuto «mettere in ombra tecnicamente tutte le famose strade alpine». Perfino gli opprimenti tempi di crisi non erano riusciti a frenare il tempestoso sviluppo del traffico. La quantità di autovetture in Austria era raddoppiata, dal 1924 al 1930, fino a raggiungere 17.350 (nel 1986 erano 2,6 milioni) ed in Germania si era quasi triplicata fino a raggiungere circa 650.000. I tedeschi inoltre, rappresentavano il 53% degli 1,8 milioni di ospiti stranieri in Austria.

La costruzione della strada alpina del Großglockner ci dà anche un'idea delle condizioni sociali del tempo: le paghe settimanali per

48 ore lavorative erano fra i 52 scellini (manovali qualificati) e i 75 scellini (capomastri), senza aggiunte. Il costo, al chilo, del pane nero era 58 centesimi di scellino, della carne di manzo 3,60 scellini e del burro sei scellini. Una sigaretta costava tre centesimi, un panino sette, un uovo 14, mezzo litro di birra 48 e una chilowattora di corrente elettrica 70 centesimi. Per un litro di benzina super si pagava uno scellino.

Alcuni stipendi mensili di questi anni come paragone: il Presidente della Repubblica 3913 scellini, professori di scuola media col maggior grado di retribuzione 730 scellini ed impiegati pubblici col minor grado di retribuzione 137 scellini. D'altra parte però, il Presidente della Repubblica avrebbe dovuto spendere due redditi mensili per l'autovettura del ceto sociale medio elevato più popolare in Austria, lo «Steyr Hunderter», una quattro cilindri con 1,2 litri di cilindrata, 32 CV, 100 Km/h di velocità massima e fra i nove e i 10,5 litri di consumo di benzina. Perfino l'utilitaria di piccola cilindrata più a buon mercato costava più di 5000 scellini - comprensibile se si considera la quantità minima di autovetture a quel tempo.

## In te domine speravi

La sera del 2 Agosto del 1935 un enorme fuoco dai 2571 m della «Edelweißspitze» annunciò il termine della costruzione della strada alpina. Un comunicato stampa per l'inaugurazione del 3 Agosto riportò le seguenti cifre iponenti:

La strada alpina del Großglockner misurava sei metri di larghezza e 58,5 Km di lunghezza, 1,8 Km di strada panoramica dal Fuschertörl fino alla Edelweißspitze e 8,7 Km di strada fra i ghiacciai dal Guttal alla Franz-Josefs-Höhe. Vennero impiegati 33,4 ettari di superficie stradale e di parcheggio, costruiti 67 ponti, scavate due

gallerie (Hochtor 311 metri e Mittertörl 117 metri) cablati 48 Km di telefono stradale con 24 punti per chiamate d'emergenza e costruiti 28 parcheggi nei punti di maggior effetto dal lato paesaggistico.

Quest'opera costò 25,8 milioni di scellini, 200.000 scellini in meno di quanto preventivato. Come paragone: un ponte sul Danubio, costruito anch'esso durante la metà degli Anni Trenta a Vienna (il «Reichsbrücke» crollato nel 1976) costò 24 milioni. La somma di 25,8 milioni per la costruzione corrispondeva al 5% circa del volume d'investimento austriaco del 1935.

Purtroppo la costruzione della strada alpina e la sua manutenzione costarono anche la vita a 20 persone. In loro memoria è stata eretta la cappella al Fuschertörl progettata da Clemens Holzmeister. Quando alcuni operai, nell'estate del 1933, scavarono il Hochtor, trovarono una moneta del tempo di Maria Teresa fra i detriti del pendio sul versante settentrionale. L'iscrizione sulla moneta (in te domine speravi - in te, o Signore, sperai) fu fatta incidere da Wallack sui portali del Hochtor - come ringraziamento per la riuscita dell'opera malgrado tutti i problemi. Ciò si può naturalmente anche prendere come riferimento di quanto i tempi duri incrementino la fiducia in Dio.

La strada alpina del Großglocker superò la sua prima prova già il 4 Agosto del 1935, il giorno dopo la sua inaugurazione: 75 piloti si presentarono a Fusch alla partenza della «Prima corsa internazionale del Glockner», di 19,5 Km e 1.600 metri scarsi in altezza fino al Fuschertörl. La vittoria su questa strada di sabbia spianata (solo nel 1939 fu asfaltata e resa priva di polvere l'intera strada) fu dell'italiano Mario Tadini su Alfa Romeo (categoria di macchina da corsa di 2000 ccm) in 14:42,74 minuti (79,6 Km/h).

I piloti e la stampa tributarono in seguito grandi elogi al costruttore Wallack: la strada era «diretta in modo eccezionale...assolutamente sicura per corse molto veloci... costruita in modo ideale e di prim'ordine...favolosa...» e secondo l'opinione del «Guardian» britannico «una prestazione tecnica di alto valore».

Da tale prestazione tecnica trae profitto fino ad oggi anche l'industria automobilistica. La strada alpina del Großglockner è sin dalla sua inaugurazione nel 1935 il circuito classico dei test per le prove di motori e freni. Se di quando in quando «strisciano» su e giù per la montagna dei veicoli «lenti» con strane costruzioni, rimorchi singolari e segnali luminosi ad intermittenza accesi, vuol dire che una ditta automobilistica sta cercando di perfezionare la sicurezza tecnica del veicolo.

*Blossoming of the fruit trees in Heiligenblut · Bloei van de fruitbomen in Heiligenblut · Arbres fruitiers en fleurs à Heiligenblut · Fioritura degli alberi da frutta a Heiligenblut.*

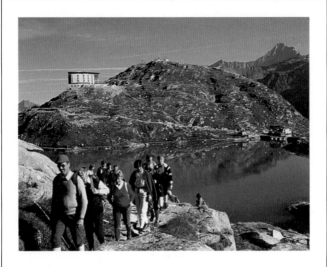

## Mit den Bergbahnen Uttendorf-Weißsee in das Wanderparadies des Nationalparks Hohe Tauern

*Unter den vielen bereits seit Jahren bekannten Ausflugszielen gibt es auch heute noch Regionen, die der Gast aber auch der „Einheimische" kennenlernen sollte. Besonders im Rahmen des Nationalparks Hohe Tauern wurde das Bewußtsein der unberührten und erhaltenswerten Natur in der Bevölkerung wieder stärker. Die Nationalpark-Region Uttendorf-Weißsee im Salzburger Land eröffnet die Begegnung mit der Natur und führt weg vom Massentourismus in eine Landschaft, deren eigenartiger Reiz von hochmoorähnlichen Landstrichen, der Almrauschblüte und glasklaren Gebirgsseen geprägt wird.*

*Von Uttendorf aus führt eine mautfreie Panoramastraße durch das wildromantische Stubachtal zur Einseilumlaufbahn Rudolfshütte, die den Besucher sanft-schwebend dem Erlebnis Natur näher bringt. Hier ist der Ausgangspunkt für Spaziergänger und Wanderbegeisterte ebenso wie für Bergfreunde und Alpinisten. Das Weißseegebiet bietet alle alpinen Naturschönheiten, die Sie sich von einem Bergausflug erwarten, und es ist sicher, daß Ihr Besuch ein Erlebnis wird.*

*Entdecken Sie also eine jener noch stillen österreichischen Regionen, in der Sie Ihr Urlaubsziel – nämlich die Erholung – ganz sicher finden werden. Die Bergbahnen Uttendorf-Weißsee garantieren eine reibungslose, wartezeitfreie Beförderung; die Landschaft aber – das eigentliche Erlebnis – braucht in dieser Region nicht beworben zu werden, die Natur spricht für sich.*

*Nationalpark Hohe Tauern: Alle reden davon – wir bringen Sie hin!*

*Nähere Informationen gibt es im Büro der Bergbahnen – Telefon 06563/593 – oder beim Fremdenverkehrsverband Uttendorf.*

In estate l'automobilista è colpito anche da ciclisti che mettono alla prova il loro rendimento. Ogni anno, e questo dal 1949, la tappa del Glockner sul Hochtor è il culmine del Giro dell'Austria. I rendimenti massimi dei «giganti della strada maestra» si possono stimare contando che il tempo minimo di salita da Heiligenblut al Hochtor (52,02 minuti) corrisponde ad una media oraria di 16,1 chilometri.

## Protezione della natura e tecnica

Ancor prima che cominciasse la costruzione di questa strada alpina, che avrebbe dovuto «mettere in ombra tutte le strade alpine» secondo la visione di Wallack, già cresceva la resistenza contro il progetto da parte di coloro che si impiegavano per la protezione della natura. Nel 1918 infatti, l'industriale del legno, il carinziano Albrecht Wirth, aveva comprato un terreno di quasi 41 Km quadrati intorno alla Pasterze e l'aveva regalato alla Lega Alpina a patto che questo paesaggio delle Alte Alpi «rimanesse in eterno un territorio protetto da sottrarre all'industria speculativa alpina per turisti». Eppure la strada alpina del Großglockner doveva arrivare proprio alla Franz-Josefs-Höhe, un punto al confine con questo territorio protetto che offre una vista unica sui ghiacciai più armoniosi dell'Austria e sulla montagna più alta.

I protettori della natura non riuscirono ad imporsi. Wallack però per fortuna, non era solo costruttore di strade ma anche un eccellente alpinista con un acuto senso per la protezione della natura. Perciò attribuì una priorità alla cura del paesaggio durante la costruzione: riuscì ad imporre che la vegetazione del paesaggio fosse prelevata con cautela e venisse usata come verde per le scarpate e le «cicatrici« provocate durante la costruzione. Fece anche piantare dei giardini in differenti altitudini e zone climatiche per poter coltivare

quella vegetazione biotopicamente tollerabile che più tardi sarebbe servita per l'ampiamento e la modernizzazione di questa strada.

Cartelli lungo la strada alpina del Großglockner pregano ripetutamente i turisti di osservare la protezione della natura. Gli amanti della natura rispettano queste norme perché il forte traffico turistico grava comunque sulla natura nella quale, con la quale e della quale noi tutti viviamo.

Tutto ciò spiega perché la strada alpina del Großglockner si inserisce con discrezione nel Parco Nazionale degli Alti Tauri, il quale è attraversato dalla strada fra il Fuschertörl e il Hochtor come anche dal Guttal fino alla Franz-Josefs-Höhe.

La disposizione di questa strada alpina tiene testa in tal modo, secondo l'opinione dell'internazionalmente stimato professore di architettura, l'austriaco Friedrich Achleitner, anche ai criteri della nostra sensibile epoca: «sebbene essa sia ancora senz'altro un prodotto di metodi manuali, il terreno quindi, non ancora violentato dal rigoroso impiego di macchinari, la bellezza paesaggistica e la sua utilizzazione erano al centro dell'interesse. Ciò è una prova che interessi economici e l'ingegno tecnico non debbano per forza distruggere il paesaggio.»

# Tracce millenarie

Questa strada sul Hochtor ed attraverso il nucleo del Parco Nazionale degli Alti Tauri segue tracce antichissime, leggibili su imponenti reperti. Nel «Beindlkar» a sud del Mittertörl (al Km 31) fu trovato, vicino alla strada, un pugnale di bronzo del 17. secolo avanti Cristo. A circa due ore di cammino a valle di questo punto, un taglialegna trovò un frammento di un collare celtico del 5. secolo avanti Cristo. Durante la costruzione del Hochtor (al Km 33,4) alcuni operai trovarono una statuetta raffigurante Ercole e frammenti di una lampada romana di argilla del periodo intorno alla nascita di Cristo - sono questi, insieme ad altri ritrovamenti di ugual valore nelle valli ad ambedue i lati del Hochtor, una prova che i Romani utilizzarono questo valico alpino. Centinaia di chiodi, ferri di cavallo, speroni e parti metalliche di imbrigliature ritrovate lungo la strada alpina del Großglockner, dimostrano un vivo commercio attraverso questo valico durante il Medioevo. Sappiamo inoltre da vecchi documenti, che a quel tempo, il 10% circa del commercio lontano fra il centro commerciale di Venezia e il territorio della Germania meridionale e la Boemia si svolgeva passando sul Hochtor.

*"Harpfen" – a rural drying frame for grass · „Harpfen" – een constructie om gras op te drogen · Séchage de l'herbe sur les «Harpfen» · Il «Harpfen», una struttura contadina secca per l'erba.*

Per l'automobilista odierno è praticamente impossibile immaginare che il commercio transalpino si svolgesse allora principalmente in inverno. Eppure la maggior parte dei commercianti avevano come «occupazione secondaria» quella del contadino ed in inverno si occupavano dei loro campi. Il commercio invernale sul Hochtor lo dimostrano anche i chiodi spinati ritrovati in grandi quantità lungo la strada – sono questi, in un certo senso, i precursori degli odierni pneumatici chiodati del traffico automobilistico invernale. Attraverso il Hochtor, verso sud, passarono però anche tristi trasporti. Durante l'ingrandimento della strada alpina del Großglockner nella «Hexenküche» (Km 23,5) si trovarono delle catene per detenuti del 17. secolo. A quel tempo infatti, criminali e cacciatori di frodo venivano condannati spesso alla galera a Salisburgo e, incatenati fra loro, venivano condotti attraverso il Hochtor fino a Venezia. Cartelli in più punti della strada alpina del Großglockner richiamano l'attenzione sulla strada romana riconoscibile per lunghi tratti parallelamente all'autostrada. Questi resti di una strada larga fino a quattro metri e concepita in maniera oltremodo ingegnosa, derivano naturalmente dal Medioevo, dal periodo aureo del commercio transalpino compiuto sui dorsi dei cavalli e dall'estrazione dell'oro negli Alti Tauri.

*76/77 ◀ The road along the summit in late summer (left) and in spring · Het hoogste deel van de route in de nazomer (links) en in het voorjaar · La route des sommets à la fin de l'été (à gauche) et au printemps · Il percorso al vertice ad estate inoltrata (sinistra) ed in primavera.*

Lo scrittore romano Polibio (200-120 avanti Cristo ca.) riferisce di ciò che già ai suoi tempi aveva attratto la gente in questo luogo selvaggio delle Alpi: «L 'oro a due piedi di profondità in parte oro puro grande quanto un fagiolo» ed in tali quantità che «il prezzo dell'oro in Italia scese subito di un terzo». Alla metà del 16. secolo l'estrazione dell'oro, principalmente nelle montagne ad est della strada alpina del Großglockner - ancor'oggi chiamate «Gruppo delle montagne dorate» - ebbe il suo culmine con rendite annuali fino a circa 870 Kg di oro. Era quasi il 10% della produzione di oro del mondo allora conosciuto, è per questo che a quel tempo Salisburgo veniva chiamata anche «il piccolo Perù del vecchio mondo».

L' occhio esperto riesce a riconoscere ancora oggi, nella zona del Hochtor, i materiali di scarico dell'estrazione dell'oro del periodo medievale. Al Km 32,6 il cartello «Knappenstube» richiama l'attenzione sull'ingresso di una galleria in rovina vicino alla strada del Glockner.

Sul Hochtor corre la frontiera fra le due regioni austriache, la Carinzia e Salisburgo. Questa frontiera naturale sulla cresta montuosa delle Alpi racchiude anch'essa una parte notevole di storia.

## Uomini popolano le Alpi

Quando nel 7. secolo i Baiuvari popolarono in modo rado le valli a nord dei Tauri, dovettero strappare pascoli e campi alle foreste. Nomi come Hochmais lungo la strada alpina del Großglockner (Km 21,6) o Maishofen, sono chiari riferimenti al faticoso dissodamento (in antico alto tedesco meizan = dissodare, falciare). Fecero lo stesso gli Slavi che a quel tempo si stabilirono nel Mölltal, come è da ricavare dal nome del campo Laserzen (laz = dissodamento) o dal villaggio Stribach (strebsti = dissodare). Assolutamente inutilizzabile per l'agricoltura e perciò solo punto d'orientamento era il «Naßfeld» nella rampa a nord della strada alpina del Großglockner (Km 26) ma anche i «Mesenaten» (Km 35) a sud del Hochtor (mizinat = paludoso quindi nuovamente «Naßfeld», campo umido).

Con ciò si apre un'imponente dimensione storica che ci riempie di profondo rispetto: contadini e pastori coltivarono gli Alti Tauri all'incirca 1400 anni fa. Dall'impressionante campanile tardo-romanico del villaggio del Glockner Fusch, è da stimare che i padri spirituali si stabilirono nelle colonie alpine nel 12. o 13. secolo. L'obbligo scolastico arrivò nelle valli alpine solamente al tempo dell'imperatrice Maria Teresa (1740-1780). Solo un secolo più tardi vi si stabilì anche un medico.

*Drive up to the chapel at the Fuschertörl · Oprit naar de kapel bij het ◀ 80/81 Fuschertörl · Montée à la chapelle du Fuschertörl · Salita alla cappella del Fuschertörl.*

**79**

...no negli Alti Tauri anche uomini che, in ...ato delle Alte Alpi, presumevano la sede di spi-...e preparatrici di temporali e mostri leggendari. Se prima ...erano cimentati su queste alture solo cacciatori e pastori, talvolta anche botanici che cercavano erbe medicinali nella farmacia di Dio, così ora cominciarono improvvisamente ad interessarsi a queste montagne anche studiosi di scienze naturali. Ciò diede lo spunto per l'apertura verso le Alpi e la scalata delle cime.

Nell'anno 1799 il vescovo principe carinziano Franz Xaver conte Salm-Reifferscheid organizzò una spedizione di 30 persone e 13 cavalli per superare il Großglockner. La spedizione fallì a causa del maltempo, ma un anno più tardi una grande spedizione di 62 persone e 16 cavalli riuscì ad arrivare fino alla Adlersruhe nel giro di due giorni, dalla quale poi cinque uomini giunsero fino alla cima più alta dei Tauri. Ambedue le spedizioni furono finanziate dal conte Salm-Reifferscheid di tasca propria - con una somma con la quale oggi sarebbe possibile a 20 persone compiere una spedizione di tre settimane nell'Himalaja.

## Masse di neve alpine

Nelle stazioni per il pedaggio donne in decorativi costumi tradizionali richiedono purtroppo una certa somma dai visitatori della strada alpina del Großglockner, in tal modo, chi paga le tasse non è costretto a pagare per la manutenzione.

Proprio una strada alpina necessita di un grande impiego di mezzi tecnici e finanziari a causa della troppo spesso sottovalutata forza distruttrice di neve e gelo, delle valanghe, delle frane e delle cadute massi. Con tali mezzi è possibile garantire la manutenzione della carreggiata e della costruzione ed agli ospiti un viaggio sicuro in una zona esposta in modo particolare a clima e paesaggio.

Durante l'inverno cadono in regola cinque metri di neve sul tratto più alto della strada alpina (fra i 2300 e i 2500 metri di altezza sul livello del mare). Il modo in cui tale massa si posa non dipende certo solo dalla quantità della neve. Piuttosto è da considerare che in tali altitudini non c'è mai calma di vento e la sua velocità arriva ad essere di tre volte superiore rispetto alla media nelle valli, con punte fino a 130 Km/h. Ciò spiega i notevoli trasporti di neve e la formazione di enormi cornici di neve e ghiaccio anche in estate.

Ora è chiaro come mai la strada alpina del Großglockner passi anche a luglio attraverso parti innevate. Bufere di neve in inverno hanno accumulato la neve al di sopra della strada, nel 1975 rag-

Rotation plows eliminate up to 800,000 m³ of snow annually · Rotatieploegen verwijderen soms wel 800.000 m³ sneeuw per jaar · Les machines à dispositif rotatif enlèvent chaque année jusq'à 800.000 m³ de neige · Gli spartineve a rotazione rimuovono annualmente fino a 800.000 m³.

giunsero l'altezza record di 21 metri - una gola come fra grattacieli di una grande città.

Lo sviluppo della tecnica lo si riconosce anche dallo sgombero della neve. 350 uomini spalarono, dal 1935 al 1937, 250.000 metri cubi di neve in circa 70 giorni, si poté così liberare una corsia della strada. Gli spartineve a rotazione ideati da Wallack compiono, dal 1953, l'opera di circa 1000 spalatori. Solo cinque spartineve a rotazione e 30 uomini sgomberano 600.000 metri cubi di neve nel giro di 25 giorni dall'intera area stradale inclusi i parcheggi. Il record di sgombero risale al 1975 con 800.000 metri cubi di neve che avrebbero potuto riempire un treno merci lungo 250 Km.

I pedaggi non nutrono quindi nessun apparato amministrativo burocratico, assicurano piuttosto l'impiego del meglio della tecnica per poter offrire ai visitatori della strada alpina del Großglockner un'esperienza turistica eccezionale.

## La Pasterze

I visitatori della Franz-Josefs-Höhe non dovrebbero assolutamente lasciarsi sfuggire un'esperienza unica in Europa: la passeggiata senza pericoli né fatiche sul ghiaccio della Pasterze che misura fino a 300 metri di spessore, 20 Km quadrati di superficie ed ha un volume di due Km cubi circa. Dal parcheggio Freiwandeck parte una funivia, esistente dal 1963, che scende 143 metri fino al margine quasi della Pasterze. Con pochi passi si raggiunge un quadrilatero recintato su un ghiacciaio sul quale scorrono mormorando piccoli torrenti in dozzine di rivoletti. Il visitatore può essere partecipe qui di una tappa dell'enorme ciclo dell'acqua: il sole scioglie il ghiacciaio ed intacca fortemente la sua sostanza. Salendo ancora molti chilometri su per il ghiacciaio, si trova la neve anche in estate. Si tratta qui del «territorio fertile» del ghiacciaio il cui confine con il «territorio consumato» (ghiaccio privo di neve) scorre a circa 2800 metri sul livello del mare.

Alture a circa 3000 metri e più hanno due volte e mezzo più precipitazioni che a valle, il 90% sono di neve - dai sei ai dieci metri l'anno. Questa massa si comprime fino ad arrivare a 20 - 50 cm di spessore sotto l'influsso del calore e l'avvicendarsi di scioglimento e congelamento trasformandosi in ghiaccio nel giro di 15 anni.

La scienza ha scoperto solo due secoli fa la relazione fra il clima e la nascita dei ghiacciai. Prima la gente devota trovava spiegazioni che fino ad oggi persistono come leggende. Laddove oggi la Pasterze riempie un'enorme valle si estendevano un tempo pascoli rigogliosi: gli alpini si diedero ad una gozzoviglia senza limiti e portarono al limite estremo i loro atti sacrileghi giocando con palle di burro e birilli di formaggio e lasciando predicare il sacerdote davanti ai banchi vuoti della chiesa. Dio, in una furia senza limiti, mandò un terribile temporale che sciacquò via tutte queste attività peccaminose. In tal modo le masse d'acqua si trasformarono in una corrente di ghiaccio perché il luogo della dissolutezza fosse coperto per sempre e mostrasse agli uomini dove porta l'empietà.

## Attrazione per milioni

Wallack stimò nel 1924 che bisognava contare annualmente su 40.000 visitatori della strada alpina del Großglockner. All'inizio della costruzione, nel 1930, Wallack contò su 120.000 visitatori - ebbe così contro di sé le critiche canzonatorie degli esperti scettici. Ma nel 1938 – nel terzo anno di piena attività – si contarono già 98.000 veicoli e 275.000 visitatori. Oggi passano in media 280.000 veicoli l'anno sulla strada alpina del Großglockner. Agli inizi degli Anni Cinquanta si cominciò con l'ingrandimento per tenere testa alla sicurezza ed alle esigenze di comodità del viaggio. La strada fu allargata perciò da sei ad almeno 7,5 metri e, nei tratti più esigenti dal punto di vista della guida, fino a tre corsie, i raggi delle curve furono allargati da dieci ad almeno 15 metri ed ampliata l'offerta delle aree di parcheggio da 800 a 4000 posti macchina.

Franz Wallack si pose come obiettivo di costruire negli Alti Tauri una strada che tenesse testa a tutte le altre strade alpine. Da allora, approssimativamente 40 milioni di visitatori confermano che Wallack ha raggiunto il suo obiettivo con la sua meravigliosa strada delle Alpi.

*This coin was found near the work area at the Hochtor · Deze munt werd gedurende de bouw van het Hochtor gevonden · Cette pièce de monnaie fut trouvée lors de travaux au Hochtor · Questa moneta fu trovata durante i lavori sul Hochtor.*

# Points of Interest along the Großglockner Alpine Highway · Bezienswaardigheden langs de Großglockner-route · Curiosités le long de la route du Großglockner · Particolarità lungo la strada alpina del Großglockner

| km | Altitude Hoogte Altitude Altezza | Name Naam Nom Nome | Description Beschrijving Description Descrizione |
|---|---|---|---|
| 0 | 757 | Bruck | Beginning of the Großglockner Alpine Highway · Begin van de Großglockner-route · Début de la route du Großglockner · Inizio della strada alpina del Großglockner |
| 3,2 | 790 | Vorderwald | Splendid old Pinzgauer-style farm · Twee prachtige bijeenstaande Pinzgauer boerderijen · Magnifique vieille ferme du Pinzgau à deux bâtiments · Splendido vecchio podere del Pinzgau |
| 7,3 | 805 | Fusch | Late-Romanesque church steeple · Laat-romaanse kerktoren · Clocher de la fin de l'époque romane · Campanile tardo-romanico |
| 10,1 | 863 | Embachkapelle | Beginning of the mountain portion · Begin van de bergweg · Début de la route de montagne · Inizio del tratto montano |
| 11,7 | 1021 | Bärenschlucht | Frequently large remains of avalanches · Vaak resten van grote lawines · Imposants restes d'avalanche · Spesso grandi resti di valanghe |
| 14,5 | 1145 | Mauthaus Ferleiten | Toll booth, beginning of the natural conservation zone · Tolkantoor, begin van het natuurbeschermingsgebied · Péage, début de la zone à la nature protégée · Posto pedaggio, inizio della zona di protezione della natura |
| 19,3 | 1620 | Parkplatz Piffkar | Excellent spot for photography · Uitstekend geschikt om te foto's te maken · Excellent emplacement pour prendre des photos · Eccezionale punto fotografico |
| 32,5 | 2450 | Knappenstube | Recognizable remains from gold mining · Duidelijk zichtbare overblijfselen van de goudmijnen · Restes visibles de l'exploitation des mines d'or · Resti visibili dell'estrazione dell'oro |
| 33,4 | 2503 | Parkplatz Hochtor | Location where a Hercules statue and a Roman clay lamp were found · Vindplaats van een Hercules-beeldje en een Romeinse lamp · Endroit où furent trouvées une statuette d'hercule et une lampe en argile romaine · Punto di ritrovamento della statuetta di Ercole e della lampada di argilla romana |
| 37,7 | 2099 | Tauerneck | Photography spot for the Großglockner and Zlamitzen curves · Goede plaats om de Großglockner en de Zlamitzen-haarspeldbochten te fotograferen · Emplacement pour prendre des photos du Großglockner et des lacets des «Zlamitzen» · Punto fotografico per il Großglockner e «Zlamitzenkehren» |
| 40 | 1859 | Guttal | Turn off for the glacier road · Begin van de gletsjerweg · Bifurcation de la route des glaciers · Svincolo strada di ghiacciaio |
| 41,9 | 1930 | Parkplatz Kasereck | Excellent panoramic- and photography spot, remains of the "Roman road" · Mooi uitzichtspunt en goede plek om te fotograferen, resten van de „Romeinse weg" · Magnifique point de vue et emplacement pour prendre des photos, restes de la «voie romaine» · Punto panoramico e fotografico eccezionale, resti della «strada romana» |

| km | m | Location | Description |
|---|---|---|---|
| 43,9 | 1700 | Mauthaus Heiligenblut | Toll booth · Tolkantoor · Péage · Posto pedaggio |
| 44,6 | 1620 | Wegscheider | An old farm on the valley side, "Harpfen" – ladder-like frame for the drying of hay on the mountain side · In het dal een oude boerderij, aan de kant van de berg een "Harpfen" (een rek om hooi te drogen) · Vers la vallée, ancienne ferme, vers la montagne, «Harpfen», pour sécher l'herbe · Vecchio podere a valle, «Harpfen» per seccare il fieno a monte |
| 45,6 | 1514 | Kehre 26 | Turn off to the Fleißtal, view of the "Sonnblick" · Zijweg naar het Fleißtal, blik op de „Hohe Sonnblick" · Bifurcation pour la Fleißtal, vue du «Sonnblick» · Svincolo per il Fleißtal, veduta del «Sonnblick» |
| 47,8 | 1301 | Heiligenblut | Famous Gothic church · Beroemde gotische kerk · Célèbre église gothique · Famosa chiesa gotica |

**„Gletscherstraße" – Glacier road beginning at Guttal · Gletsjerweg vanaf Guttal · Route des glaciers à partir de Guttal · Strada di ghiacciaio a partire da Guttal**

| km | m | Location | Description |
|---|---|---|---|
| 5,3 | 2131 | Parkplatz Glocknerhaus I | Beginning of the "Glacier Path" via the Pasterze to the Franz–Josefs–Höhe · Begin van de „Gletsjerweg" over de Pasterze naar de Franz–Josefs–Höhe · Début du «chemin du glacier» menant à la Franz–Josefs–Höhe par la Pasterze · Inizio del «Cammino del ghiacciaio» attraverso la Pasterze fino alla Franz-Josefs-Höhe |
| 8,7 | 2369 | Parkplatz Freiwandeck | Excellent panoramic and photography spot in front of the Großglockner and Pasterze · Schitterend uitzicht op de Großglockner en de Pasterze-gletsjer · Excellent point de vue et emplacement pour prendre de photos face au Großglockner et à la Pasterze · Punto panoramico e fotografico eccezionale davanti al Großglockner e Pasterze |

| km | m | Location | Description |
|---|---|---|---|
| 21,6 | 1850 | Parkplatz Hochmais | Edge of the timber line, photography spot · Boomgrens, plek om te fotograferen · Limite de la forêt, emplacement pour prendre des photos · Confine del bosco, punto fotografico |
| 23,5 | 2058 | Hexenküche (Unternalfeld) | Landslide area · Bergverschuivingsgebied · Zone d'éboulement · Territorio di frana |
| 24,2 | 2116 | Kehre 10, Hexenküche | Excellent place for photography · Prima plek om te fotograferen · Excellent emplacement pour prendre des photos · Eccezionale punto fotografico |
| 25 | 2240 | Edelweißwand | Vestiges of the "Roman Road" (4 curves) · Resten van de „Romeinse weg" (4 haarspeldbochten) · Restes de la «voie romaine» (4 lacets) · Resti della «strada romana» (4 curve) |
| 26,9 | 2394 | Parkplatz Fuschertörl I | Turn off to the Edelweißspitze (1,8 km.) · Zijweg naar de Edelweißspitze (1,8 km) · Bifurcation pour la Edelweißspitze (1,8 km) · Svincolo per la Edelweißspitze (1,8 km) |
|  | 2571 | Edelweißspitze | Highest point on the Großglockner Highway, excellent panoramic- and photography spot · Hoogste punt van de Glocknerweg, prachtig uitzicht · Point le plus élevé de la route du Großglockner, magnifique point de vue et emplacement pour prendre des photos · Punto più alto della strada alpina del Glockner, punto panoramico e fotografico eccezionale |
| 27,4 | 2428 | Parkplatz Fuschertörl II | Excellent panoramic and photography spot · Schitterend uitzichtspunt, prima plek om te fotograferen · Point de vue et excellent emplacement pour prendre des photos · Punto panoramico e fotografico eccezionale |
| 29,3 | 2262 | Parkplatz Fuscherlacke | Recognizable remains of the "Roman Road" · Overblijfselen van de „Romeinse weg" · Restes visibles de la «voie romaine» · Resti visibili della «strada romana» |

# The "Hohe Tauern" National Park

The Alps determine the character of Austria's landscape, a living space that has formed the people of this country. A part of that area is preserved in its originality for present and future generations.

The "Hohe Tauern" National Park ist situated in one of the most beautiful regions of the Eastern Alps, an area of 121,000 hectars of almost untouched nature in the center of the "Old World", bearing witness of the unique characteristic features of the Austrian provinces of Carinthia and Salzburg.

The central zone of the National Park is formed by the alpine wilderness region. High mountain ranges, with Großglockner and Großvenediger, steep walls of rock, eternal ice and rushing glacier brooks determine the monumental character of this landscape.

Man has contributed to form the peripheral zone of the National Park. Alpine pastures, mountain meadows and protection forests give evidence of what man has created in harmony with nature for hundreds of years. These will be cultivated an protected in future.

The "Hohe Tauern" National Park is freely accessible for visitors having respect for the flora and fauna, and for the unique natural landscape of this region.

# Het Nationale Park „Hohe Tauern"

De Alpen bepalen het beeld van het Oostenrijkse landschap en hebben hun stempel gedrukt op de mensen die in dit land wonen. Een deel van dit gebied is in zijn oorspronkelijke toestand voor ons en voor de toekomstige generaties behouden gebleven.

Het nationale park „Hohe Tauern" (Hoge Tauern) bestaat uit een van de mooiste en meest ongerepte streken van de oostelijke Alpen. Het is een 121.000 hectare groot stuk natuur in het hart van Europa, dat een indukwekkend beeld geeft van het unieke karakter van de Oostenrijkse provincies Karinthië en Salzburg.

De kern van het nationale park wordt gevorm door woest hooggebergte. Machtige bergen, met als hoogste toppen de Großglockner en de Großvenediger, stijle rotswanden, eeuwige sneeuw en bruisende beekjes bepalen het monumentale karakter van dit stuk pure natuur.

In de randgebieden van het nationale park zijn de eerste menselijke invloeden zichtbaar. Almen, bergweiden en schermbossen zijn stille getuigen van het harmonische samenleven van mens en natuur. Vaak eeuwenoud worden ze nu verder verzorgd en onderhouden.

*88/89 ◖ Drive to the Franz-Josefs-Höhe (left) and to the Freiwandeck parking area · Weg naar de Franz-Josefs-Höhe en parkeerterrein Freiwandeck (links) · Montée à la Franz- Josefs-Höhe (à gauche) et parking Freiwandeck · Percorso verso la Franz-Josefs-Höhe (sinistra) e parcheggio Freiwandeck.*

Het nationale park „Hohe Tauern" is vrij toegankelijk voor bezoekers met een groot besef van verantwoordelijkheid. Wie de plantenen dierenwereld respecteert en de natuur ontziet kan dit magnifieke landschap te voet ontdekken.

## Le Parc National «Hohe Tauern»

Le paysage autrichien est marqué par les Alpes, espace vital qui a formé les hommes de cette pays. L'originalité d'une partie de cette région est conservée pour les générations présentes et futures.

Le Parc National «Hohe Tauern» – 121.000 hectares de nature intacte au coeur de «l'Ancien Continent» – est situé dans un des plus beaux sites des Alpes orientales et il est la preuve éclatante de l'originalité de la Land de Salzbourg et de la Carinthie.

Une région sauvage très ancienne forme la zone centrale du Parc National, composée de massifs imposants avec les sommets du Großglockner et du Großvenediger, de parois abruptes, neiges éternelles et torrents grondants.

La périphérie du Parc National a été façonnée par l'homme. Alpages, patûrages alpestres, forêts protégées témoignent du travail de l'homme au cours des siècles en parfaite communion avec la nature. Ils continueront d'être soignés et conservés.

Le Parc National «Hohe Tauern» est librement accessible à tous les visiteurs conscients de leur responsabilité envers la flore, la faune et la nature.

# Il Parco Nazionale «Hohe Tauern»

Le Alpi determinano il carattere del paesaggio austriaco, spazio vitale che ha formato l'uomo di questo paese. Una parte di questo paesaggio è conservato nella propria originalità per l'uomo di oggi e per le generazioni future.

Il Parco Nazionale «Hohe Tauern» (Alti Tauri) è situato in una delle più belle regioni delle Alpi Orientali, 121.000 ettari di natura ampiamente intatta nel centro del «Continente Antico», dimostrando in modo impressionante il carattere inconfondibile delle due regioni austriache, la Carinzia e Salisburgo.

La zona centrale del Parco Nazionale è formata dalla regione primitiva delle Alpi, con grandi montagne, superate dalle cime del Großglockner e Großvenediger, pareti rocciose ripide, ghiaccio eterno e torrenti mormoranti, che determinano il carattere monumentale di questo paesaggio.

La zona periferica del Parco Nazionale è stata formata dall'uomo. Pascoli alpini e riserve forestali sono testimonianze di quanto fatto dall'uomo per secoli in armonia con la natura. Vengono coltivati e conservati perchè rimangano intatte anche in futuro.

Il Parco Nazionale «Hohe Tauern» è liberamente aperto ai visitatori consapevoli della propria responibilità. Chi ha cura della fauna, della flora e del paesaggio intatto, può visitare a piedi questa regione naturale magnifica.

**Information on the "Hohe Tauern" National Park · Informaties over het nationale park „Hohe Tauern" · Renseignements sur le Parc National «Hohe Tauern» · Informazioni sul parco nazionale «Hohe Tauern»**

General information and useful tips on vacations in the "Hohe Tauern" National Park may be obtained at the following locations:

Algemene inlichtingen en nuttige tips voor een vakantie in het nationale park „Hohe Tauern" kunt u krijgen bij:

Les organismes suivant vous fourniront des renseignements d'ordre général et des tuyaux utiles pour passer des vacances dans le Parc National «Hohe Tauern»:

Informazioni generali e suggerimenti utili concernenti le vacanze nel parco nazionale degli Alti Tauri sono disponibili presso i seguenti indirizzi:

**Nationalparkkommission Hohe Tauern**

Johann-Panzl-Straße 5, A-9971 Matrei/Osttirol, Tel. 04875/6895.

**Nationalpark-Verwaltung Kärnten**

A-9844 Heiligenblut, Tel. 04824/2525.

**Nationalpark-Verwaltung Salzburg**

A-5741 Neukirchen am Großvenediger 306, Tel. 06565/6558.

*Blossoms and butterflies from the National Park in the Glockner area · Bloesems en vlinders uit het nationale park in het Glocknergebied · Fleurs et papillons du Parc National sur le territoire du Großglockner · Fiori e farfalle del parco nazionale nel territorio del Glockner.*

## Hiking on Horseback in the National Park

At the time of the Celts and the Romans, men were already crossing the Tauern range on Horseback and in the Middle Ages, pack horses transported wine, fruit, glass, spices and silk almost 600 years long from Venice to the cold North through the passes.

Today, Hubert Sauper, „Schloßwirt"-proprietor in the beautiful Großkirchheim (a few kilometers from Heiligenblut) leads venturesome families and groups on these old mule tracks with his own horses into the solitude of the Hohe Tauern National Park – in naturally – romantic valleys, to quiet mountain lakes and babbling mountain brooks or to half- deteriorated tunnels from the time of the gold rush.

Hiking and horseback riding in untouched nature, in viewing range of the 3000 meter peaks of the National Park is just the right way to make a vacation „adventuresome".

The „Schloßwirt" National Park Hotel and Hubert Sauper can be reached under the telephone number 04825/211.

## Randonnées à cheval dans le Parc National

A l'époque des Celtes et des Romains, les hommes traversaient déjà les Tauern à dos de cheval et au Moyen Age, des mulets transportèrent pendant plus de 600 ans vin, fruits, verre, épices et soie de Venise aux froids pays du nord en passant par les cols.

Hubert Sauper, hôtelier à Großkirchheim (à quelques kilomètres de Heiligenblut), organise aujourd'hui sur ces chemins muletiers des randonnées à cheval pour familles et groupes épris d'aventure dans la solitude du Parc National «Hohe Tauern»; il leur fait découvrir des vallées d'un romantisme sauvage, de calmes lacs de montagne et des torrents grondants ou bien des galeries abandonnées de l'époque de la ruée vers l'or.

Randonnée et équitation dans une nature intacte, au pied des sommets de 3000 mètres du Parc National – on ne peut trouver mieux des vacances à la recherche de l'aventure !

On peut prendre contact avec Hubert Sauper à l'hôtel «Schloßwirt» en appelant le numéro de téléphone 04825/211.

## Escursioni a cavallo nel parco nazionale

Già al tempo dei Celti e dei Romani si attraversavano i Tauri a cavallo e, durante il Medioevo, per 600 anni, i cavalli da soma trasportarono vino, frutta, vetro, spezie e seta da Venezia al freddo nord attraverso i passi.

Hubert Sauper, albergatore nel bel Großkirchheim (ad alcuni Km da Heiligenblut) conduce, lungo le antiche mulattiere, famiglie e gruppi pieni di iniziativa con i suoi cavalli nella solitudine del parco nazionale degli Alti Tauri. Conduce in valli selvagge e romantiche, a calmi laghi alpini, a spumosi torrenti alpini o a gallerie diroccate dei tempi della febbre dell'oro.

Le escursioni e l'equitazione nella natura intatta, con le montagne del parco nazionale a vista d'occhio, sono attività ottimali per una perfetta vacanza avventurosa.

Per contattare l'albergo del parco nazionale «Schloßwirt» e Hubert Sauper: Tel. 04825/211.

# The Communities on the Glockner Highway ·
# De gemeentes langs de Glockner-route ·
# Les communes de la route du Großglockner ·
# I comuni lungo la strada del Glockner

**The numbers of the „Freytag & Berndt" hiking maps which pertain to the Glockner area can be gathered in the following community overviews under „f&b Hiking Maps".**

**De nummers van de voor het Glocknergebied belangrijke „Freytag & Berndt" wandelkaarten vindt u in het volgende gemeenteoverzicht onder „f&b-wandelkaarten".**

**Dans le texte de description des communes vous trouverez les numéros des cartes de randonnée «Freytag & Berndt» concernant la région du Großglockner.**

**I numeri delle cartine «Freytag & Berndt» riguardanti il territorio del Glockner, si trovano nei seguenti quadri riguardanti i comuni sotto: «cartine f&b».**

## Bruck an der Glocknerstraße (758 m)

The Bruck area has been populated for around 4000 years. Grave findings from Roman times along with other traces prove that

*South portal of the Hochtor (above) and view from the tunnel · Zuidelijke ingang van het Hochtor (boven) en blik vanuit de tunnel · Portail sud du Hochtor (en haut) et vue depuis le tunnel · Portale sud del Hochtor (sopra) e veduta dalla galleria.*

Bruck (the dialect form of Brücke = bridge) was a Roman base for traffic along the Hochtor. The village chronicle takes note of tragic events, for example, that Bruck was completely destroyed by fire in 1526 by a farmers' revolt and that numerous Protestants had to leave their homeland in 1731 because they refused to return to Catholicism. The divine picture „Mary on the Ice" (ca. 1500), is on the main altar of the parish church. According to legend, this statue reached Bruck on an ice floe of the Salzach River for wich this Blessed Virgin is now honored as the guardian saint of travellers.

**f&b Hiking Maps:** 10, 12, 38, 103, 122, 193, 382, 383.
**To reach higher altitudes:** Local post bus lines to the Hochtor and to Heiligenblut via the Groß-glockner Alpine Highway.

De streek rondom Bruck i reeds ca. 4000 jaar bewoond. Graven uit de Romeinse tijd bewijzen samen met andere sporen, dat Bruck (dialect voor Brücke = brug) een Romeins steunpunt was voor het verkeer over het Hochtor. De dorpskroniek vermeldt het treurige feit dat Bruck in 1526 door opstandige boeren werd platgebrand en hoe vele Protestanten in 1731 hun geboortestreek moesten verlaten, omdat ze zich niet opnieuw tot het katholicisme wilden bekeren. Op het hoogaltaar van de parochiekerk staat het genadebeeld „Maria op het ijs" (rond 1500). Volgens de legende bereikte dit beeld

Bruck op een ijsschots in de Salzach. Daarom wordt deze madonna ook wel als patrones van de reizigers vereerd.

**f&b wandelkaarten:** 10, 12, 38, 103, 122, 193, 382, 383.
**Mogelijkheden om naar boven te komen:** Postbus – lijndienst naar het „Hochtor" en naar Heiligenblut via de Großglockner- route.

La région de Bruck est peuplée depuis environ 4000 ans. Des objets trouvés dans des tombeaux remontant à l'époque romaine prouvent entre autres que Bruck (en dialecte pour Brücke – le pont) servait de base aux Romains pour le trafic qui passait par le Hochtor. La chronique du village rapporte des événements tristes; en 1526, Bruck fut brûlé par des paysans insurgés et en 1731, plusieurs protestants durent quitter leur patrie, car ils ne voulaient pas se reconvertir au catholicisme. Le maître-autel de l'église paroissiale est surmonté d'une statue de la Vierge «Marie auf dem Eis» (Vierge sur un bloc de glace). D'après la légende, cette statue est arrivée à Bruck charriée par la Salzach sur un bloc de glace; c'est la raison pour laquelle cette Vierge est vénérée comme la patronne des voyageurs.

**Cartes de randonnée f&b:** 10, 12, 38, 103, 122, 193, 382, 383.
**Moyens de transport:** Service régulier de cars de la poste pour le Hochtor et vers Heiligenblut en passant par la route du Großglockner.

La zona di Bruck è popolata da circa 4.000 anni. Reperti risalenti al tempo dei Romani confermano, insieme ad altre tracce, che Bruck (= ponte in dialetto) era una base dei Romani per il traffico attraverso il Hochtor. La cronaca del villaggio riporta tristi avvenimenti. Bruck infatti, fu incendiata nel 1526 durante una ribellione di contadini e, nel 1731, diversi protestanti dovettero lasciare le loro case poiché non volevano convertirsi al cattolicesimo. Sull' altare maggiore della parrocchia vi è l'immagine «Maria sul ghiaccio» (del 1500 circa). Secondo la leggenda, questa statua arrivò a Bruck su una lastra di ghiaccio del fiume Salzach. Per tale motivo questa Madonna viene venerata come patrona dei viaggiatori.

**Cartine f&b:** 10, 12, 38, 103, 122, 193, 382, 383.
**Mezzi di trasporto per la salita:** autobus postale di linea fino al Hochtor e a Heiligenblut sulla strada alpina del Großglockner.

**Information / Informatie / Renseignements / Informazioni:**
Fremdenverkehrsverband (Tourist Association / VVV / Office de Tourisme / Ente per il turismo) A-5671 Bruck an der Glocknerstraße, Tel. 06545/295.

## Fusch an der Glocknerstraße (805 m)

The name of this Alpine village is rooted in the Latin word „fuscus" (= dark) and thus attests for the transalpine traffic in Roman times. In the 13th century, the increasing population necessitated major clearing of land in order to promote agricultural production. Gold mining was performed in the Fusch Valley from the 16th up till the 19th century. For at least 300 years, the Pinzgauers' pilgrimage along the Hochtor to Heiligenblut begins annually on the 28th of June from the communal area of Fusch. Within this communal area, at the end of the valley from Ferleiten – the famous Rotmoos is also located, the bottom of a one-time lake, where orchids bloom in the spring.

**f&b Hiking Maps:** 12, 38, 122, 193, 382, 383.
**To reach higher altitudes:** Local post bus lines to the Hochtor and to Heiligenblut via the Großglockner Alpine Hihgway.

De naam van dit Alpendorp vindt zijn oorsprong in het Latijnse woord „fuscus" (= donker) en is dus een bewijs voor het transalpine verkeer gedurende de Romeinse tijd. In de 13e eeuw maakte het toenemen van de bevolking in dit gebied grote rodingen noodzakelijk om langbouwgrond te creëren. Tussen de 16e en de 19e eeuw werd er in het dal van Fusch goud gedolven. En sinds 300 jaar begint in het gemeentegebied van Fusch ieder jaar op 28 juni bedevaart van de inwoners van Pinzgau over het Hochtor naar Heiligenblut. Binnen de gemeentegrenzen van Fusch – in het boveneinde van het dal van Ferleiten – ligt ook het beroemde Rotmoos, de bodem van een vroeger meer, waar in het begin van de zomer orchideeën bloeien.

**f&b wandelkaarten:** 12, 38, 122, 193, 382, 383.
**Mogelijkheden om naar boven te komen:** Postbus-lijndienst naar het Hochtor en naar Heiligenblut via de Großglockner-route.

Le nom de ce village des Alpes vient du mot latin «fuscus» (sombre), ce qui prouve l'existence d'un trafic transalpin à l'époque romaine. Au XIIIème siècle, des défrichements importants furent entrepris pour encourager la production agricole par suite de l'augmentation de la population. Du XVIème au XIXème siècle, des mines d'or furent exploitées dans la vallée. Et chaque année, Fusch est le point de départ du pélerinage qui, chaque année le 28 juin, mène les habitants du Pinzgau à Heiligenblut en passant par le Hochtor. On trouve aussi dans la commune de Fusch, à la fin de la vallée de Ferleiten, da célèbre mousse rouge sur laquelle poussent des orchidées au début de l'été.

**Cartes de randonnée f&b:** 12, 38, 122, 193, 382, 383.
**Moyens de transport:** service régulier de cars de la poste pour le Hochtor et vers Heiligenblut en passant par la route du Großglockner.

Il nome di questo villaggio alpino risale al nome latino «fuscus» (= scuro) e testimonia il traffico transalpino al tempo dei Romani. Durante il 13. secolo furono necessari grandi dissodamenti al causa dell'aumento della colonizzazione e per incrementare la produzione agricola. Dal 16. al 19. secolo ci si dedicò all'estrazione dell'oro nella valle di Fusch. Da almeno 300 anni ricorrono annualmente, a partire dal 28 giugno, i pellegrinaggi degli abitanti della regione Pinzgau, nel territorio comunale di Fusch, attraverso il Hochtor fino a Heiligenblut. Nel territorio comunale di Fusch – alla fine della valle di Ferleiten – si trova anche il famoso Rotmoos, un antico letto di un lago nel quale fioriscono orchidee all'inizio dell'estate.

**Cartine f&b:** 12, 38, 122, 193, 382, 383.
**Mezzi di trasporto per la salita:** autobus postale di linea fino al Hochtor e a Heiligenblut sulla strada alpina del Großglockner.

## Information / Informatie / Renseignements / Informazioni:

Fremdenverkehrsverband (Tourist Association / VVV / Office de Tourisme / Ente per il turismo) A-5672 Fusch an der Glocknerstraße, Tel. 06546/236.

# Heiligenblut (1100 m)

The Glockner village, Heiligenblut, has been populated for over 3000 years as gold was discovered here very early. Heiligenblut is indebted to the climax of the gold mining period and the revenue from trade along the Hochtor for its splendid Gothic church from the 15th century with an aisle altar from the Michael Pacher school. After the decline of mining, it took until the end of the 19th century before first scientists and then mountain climbers incited the opening of tourism into the region.

**f&b Hiking Maps:** 12, 19, 122, 181, 193.
**To reach higher altitudes:** Schareck (2600 m.) cable car · funicular from the Franz-Josefs-Höhe to the Pasterze · local post bus lines on the Großglockner Alpine Highway to the Franz-Josefs-Höhe and along the Hochtor to Fusch.

Het Glocknerdorp Heiligenblut is al meer dan 3000 bewoond, omdat er op deze plek reeds zeer vroeg goud werd gevonden. De prachtige gotische kerk uit de 15e eeuw met een vleugelaltaar van de school van Michael Pacher stamt uit de tijd van de gootse bloei van de gouddelving en de inkomsten uit de handel over het Hochtor. Na het verval van de mijnbouw duurde het tot de 19e eeuw, voordat eerst wetenschappers en dan bergbeklimmers de toeristische ontsluiting van dit gebied inleidden.

**f&b wandelkaarten:** 12, 19, 122, 181, 193.
**Mogelijkheden om naar boven te komen:** Kabelbaan Schareck (2600 m) · kabelbaan van de Franz-Josefs-Höhe naar de Pasterze gletsjer · Postbus-lijndienst via de Großglockner-route naar de Franz-Josefs-Höhe en via het Hochtor naar Fusch.

Ce village sur la route du Großglockner est peuplé depuis plus de 3000 ans, car on y a trouvé très tôt de l'or. Heiligenblut doit sa magnifique église gothique du XVème siècle, avec retable de l'école de Michael Pacher, à l'apogée de l'exploitation des mines d'or et aux revenus du commerce. Après le déclin des mines d'or, il fallut attendre la fin du XIXème siècle pour voir scientifiques et alpinistes assurer la mise en valeur touristique de la région.